MOUNTAIN TEACHER

MOUNTAIN TEACHER

by KEN SLONE

Jesse Stuart Foundation
Ashland, Kentucky
2005

Dedication

To my loved ones: my wife Debbie
and my children, Beth and Stephen.

Cover Art by Tom J. Whitaker

ISBN: 1-931672-36-9

Book Design by Brett Nance

Published By:
Jesse Stuart Foundation
P.O. Box 669 • Ashland, KY 41105
(606) 326-1667 • JSFBOOKS.com

PREFACE

Having spent the majority of my life in education, either as a student or a teacher, and having had the opportunity to work in four different community colleges in two states, it is refreshing to read the delightful stories of another who has experienced the joys of teaching and learning in the Appalachian Mountains. Ken Slone is a native Kentuckian who has dedicated his life to teaching the students of Eastern Kentucky. A large part of his success can be attributed to his knowledge that he learns more from the students on some days than they do from him.

Ken Slone has a thorough understanding of the community college philosophy, the idea that all individuals can learn if the conditions are right. Ken consistently works hard to make the conditions suitable so students can be successful—and he has had considerable influence with students and with his faculty colleagues. Charlie Sizemore, a well-known Bluegrass musician and performer, was encouraged to attend Prestonsburg Community College (now Big Sandy Community and Technical College) by Thomas Whitaker who is known as the Greatest Appalachian Artist. Both individuals are prominently featured in *Mountain Teacher*. Sizemore, now a practicing attorney in Tennessee, gives accolades to Slone and Whitaker, and he unselfishly credits Big Sandy Community and Technical College for his many achievements.

Slone's teaching experiences have been captured in a series of stories and one can readily identify with the diversity, the challenges, and the opportunities that face mountain people. One experiences sadness when reading about the numerous educational barriers that continue to exist in areas characterized by poverty and unemployment. However, as you read *Mountain Teacher*, you will smile, occasionally you will laugh out loud, and all in all you will be proud there are many mountain teachers who believe that all students can learn and benefit from a well-rounded education.

It is rare to have the good fortune to work in such a dynamic and rewarding environment provided by the leaders of the Kentucky Community and Technical College System, and it is even more rare to cross paths with such talent and dedication that epitomizes a truly great mountain teacher, Mr. Ken Slone. Enjoy *Mountain Teacher*!

Dr. George D. Edwards, Ph.D.
President and CEO
Big Sandy Community and Technical College

INTRODUCTION

From their colonial beginnings until the middle of the twentieth century, the mountain people of Eastern Kentucky remained isolated from mainstream America. These mountaineers were not like the rural poor in other parts of America; their values were different. They did not have materialistic goals, and they placed a greater emphasis on home, family, and land. They were "make do" people who had learned their survival lessons the hard way.

The Civil War had been particularly devastating to the people of Appalachian Kentucky. Caught between warring armies, they expressed divided sentiments. The majority supported the North, but strong Confederate ties existed, too. The resulting local conflicts divided families and destroyed friendships. When the war ended, the bitter hatreds that remained continued into the twentieth century in the form of violent feuds.

Other effects of the war were less dramatic than the feuds but equally debilitating to Eastern Kentucky. By 1866, the Democrats assumed control of the state government and took revenge against their wartime opponents from the mountain counties. Not surprisingly, the quality of life in Appalachian Kentucky grew worse as schools and roads suffered from discriminatory funding.

Poverty and transportation difficulties engendered by the rough topography of the region intensified Appalachian isolation. Measured by today's standards, transportation in Appalachian Kentucky's early years ranked somewhere between difficult and impossible. Roads were inadequate, at best. In some counties the roads did not even intersect with roads from adjoining counties. The Big Sandy River usually provided the best shipping route to the outside world. However, by the twentieth century railroads reached into the mountains of Eastern Kentucky, primarily to carry out coal to heat the cities and fuel the industries of mainstream America.

Cultural factors also contributed to the region's isolation. Often the only significant contact with mainstream society came from military service. When Uncle Sam beat the drums of war, mountain boys (and sometimes girls, too) marched forth, for they were true patriots. The armed services offered them gainful employment and adventures that were re-told for a lifetime. But for the most part, Appalachians rarely traveled beyond the confines of their home counties. Their sense of being set apart was reinforced by the great feeling of inferiority imposed on "hillbillies," "ridge-runners," and "briers" by richer and better-educated mainstream Americans.

Eastern Kentucky's educational system mirrored the turbid ebb and flow of Appalachian history. During the colonial and antebellum periods of American history, Eastern Kentuckians prospered by the standards of the day, and their subsistence and barter economy supported a poorly-funded but emerging public education system. The Civil War, however, destroyed these rudimentary beginnings of an educational system in Eastern Kentucky. For several decades after the war, schools and educational opportunities were the exception rather than the rule in mountain counties where everyday folks struggled for survival and considered education a luxury.

By the early twentieth century, educational progress came in the form of more than a thousand one-room schools that dotted the hills and hollows of Eastern Kentucky. In them, teachers like Jesse Stuart and Cratis Williams helped to resurrect the region's quality of life. These teachers received little recognition and few tangible rewards. They handled eight grades in the same room and also served as nurse, counselor, janitor, playground director, and "lunchroom supervisor." In spite of the hard work and long hours, the pay was very low.

What these one-room schools lacked in "modern conveniences," they overcame with students who were willing to endure hardships in order to learn and improve themselves, and with teachers like Stuart and Williams who were dedicated champions of progress and learning.

The one-room schools were one of the greatest forces for change in Eastern Kentucky. They were, collectively, a salvation for people left outside mainstream American life by the currents of economic progress. When Cratis Williams taught the Caines Creek School in 1929, little had changed from the nineteenth century except that the teacher was paid by the county.

Teachers were often quite ingenious in equipping their school buildings. For example, a teacher from Letcher County who had no timepiece in her classroom cut notches in the door frame on the east side of the building. When the sun hit the first notch, it was time to begin school. The second mark signaled recess, and the third indicated lunch time; notches on a west window marked afternoon hours. Another cut up a calendar to help first graders learn to put the numbers in order. In many instances, the teachers spent much of their meager earnings on their school and students. "By the time I got through dressing those children and buying my materials, I never had anything left," said one former teacher. "I just might as well have been staying at home. All I was getting was experience."

9

Jesse Stuart called these long-forgotten heroes and heroines "immortal teachers." They were natural leaders who did not allow poverty to impede their love of learning. Successful one-room teachers usually made good use of the skills and interests of older students, who often helped younger students with their lessons. Advanced students also conducted drills for lower-grade classes and supervised play activities. Many former one-room school students remember these responsibilities as good learning experiences.

While the one-room schools developed, Eastern Kentucky also made modest beginnings for secondary and collegiate education, too. Berea College began in 1855. In 1887, Morehead, which had been riven by a bloody feud, became the site of a school that would become Morehead State University. The school began with a $500 gift from the state board of the Christian Church.

Other religious organizations also helped to develop and support educational institutions in Eastern Kentucky. Union College and Hazel Green Academy were both founded in 1880. Three years later Jackson Academy opened. The beginnings of Sue Bennet Memorial School were in 1887. In 1889, classes began at Cumberland College and Pikeville Collegiate Institute. In 1902, the Hindman Settlement School was established in Knott County to provide education opportunities and community service. By the early twentieth century, Eastern Kentucky had public high schools and several teacher training institutions..

As the economy of Appalachian Kentucky improved, public teacher training institutions grew at Morehead and Richmond (now Eastern Kentucky Unversity). The growth at Morehead represented the progression of these two teacher training schools. Morehead Normal School (1887-1922) was replaced by Morehead State Normal School (1922-1926), which became Morehead State Normal

School and Teachers College (1926-1930). At the end of the depression, the school emerged as Morehead State Teachers College (1948-1966). In 1966, the school became Morehead State University, and its regional neighbor, Eastern Kentucky University, achieved University status that same year.

To serve a growing regional population, Morehead State University and Eastern Kentucky University offered extension classes throughout their service region. Hard-working faculty and administrators put in a full day of work and then drove to Whitesburg, Pikeville, Prestonsburg, Maysville, Ashland, Corbin, Manchester, and other Eastern Kentucky towns to offer undergraduate and graduate classes.

To further serve the needs of Kentucky's rural population, the University of Kentucky created a community college system which became operational in 1964. The fourteen community colleges included Eastern Kentucky campuses in Ashland, Somerset, Maysville, Cumberland, and Hazard. Among the thousands of attendees were many "non-traditional" students, students over the age of twenty-five. The community colleges offered technical and career programs, as well as preparing many students to transfer to larger state schools at the end of their associate degree programs.

I moved to Kentucky in 1978 to accept a position with Morehead State University's Appalachian Development Center. Since then, I have worked with faculty from every community college in Eastern Kentucky, and I have been extremely impressed with the high quality of their training and commitment. Instructors like John Klee at Maysville Community College, George Edwards and Barbara Nicholls at Ashland Community and Technical College, and Ken Slone at Big Sandy Community and Technical College represent hundreds of fine community college teachers who have real expertise in an academic area and truly love to teach. They are a part of a long tradition of teaching excellence in Eastern Kentucky.

Some, like Ken Slone, also follow in the footsteps of forbears like Jesse Stuart and Cratis Williams by writing about their teaching experience in Eastern Kentucky. When you read *Mountain Teacher*, you will see that Slone and hundreds of other community college teachers are continuing the traditions of teaching excellence and community service that began with our region's one-room school teachers.

"Good teaching is forever," wrote Jesse Stuart, "and the teacher is immortal." That was true in Stuart's day and it is still true.

James M. Gifford, Ph.D.
CEO & Senior Editor
Jesse Stuart Foundation

MOUNTAIN TEACHER

CHAPTER ONE

Teachers and writers are, first, *absorbers*. I come from a land of storytellers where I could not help but absorb the essence of the people and places that surrounded me. The folk culture of the east Kentucky mountains is rapidly dissolving into a mass culture shaped by technology and hastened by a waning interest among mountain youth in preserving their heritage. My people were close to their families who gave them love and protection, their church which sustained their faith and gave them strength, and their neighbors who comprised a community of folks who accepted the individual—warts and all. They lived close to nature and to the land. They were farmers who raised their own food, or tobacco and apples for cash crops. Their cultural heritage is worthy of preservation through the continuation of the tradition of story telling.

My story begins near Hood's Creek, a tributary of the Big Sandy River in east Kentucky near the Johnson/Lawrence County line, twelve miles from Paintsville and five miles from Blaine. My parents met while attending a one-room school, the Slone School, located midway between their parents' farms. My father would skate to this one-room school in winter on the frozen creek, and before arriving at the school, Mom would take off the rubber galoshes her mother made her wear to protect her school shoes and hide them for safe keeping in a rock house to pick up on her way home in the afternoon.

I was born shortly after my mother and father moved back to Kentucky from Dayton, Ohio, where Dad migrated to find a factory job. For seven years he worked for the Huffy company making bicycles for the post-World War II early baby boomers. My brother Donald was born in Dayton. My mother was pregnant with me when they decided to return to their home county of Johnson. Dad's income suffered upon his return. The only job he could find outside the mines was at Mountain Tire Service, a tire shop located on Route 40, the road from Paintsville to Inez, Kentucky, and on to the West Virginia border.

Mountain Tire Service specialized in "recapping" or retreading used tires, and that was my father's job. He worked over tire molds, which at high temperatures fused new tread onto old tires. It is ironic that my father worked in Dayton to assemble new Huffy bicycles because Dad did not make enough money to afford to buy me a new Huffy. I rode a used one, but polished the chrome and scrubbed the whitewalls just as Dad did his used cars to make them seem new. My bicycle actually lasted longer than any of Dad's used cars. By the time they made it to used car lots in the mountains, they were often high-mileage vehicles bought at auction from Columbus rental fleets, vehicles that had had the odometer altered to roll back the mileage.

I was born in the Paintsville Clinic. My parents rented a little apartment in an old home in town, so that when I arrived, my father would not have such a long drive over gravel roads to take my mother to the hospital. Once I was born in 1953, we moved back to the little tenant-farmer shack near my father's parents. The house had what was called "brick" siding, an inexpensive siding made to resemble bricks. No one was ever fooled into believing this to be real bricks. Even at a distance, it was obvious that the "bricks" were fake because they were always crooked. It was impossible to install two sheets of this siding evenly enough to resemble the real thing. We had electricity, but my mother had no refrigerator to keep my milk cold, so she walked to my mamaw Slone's house to prepare my bottles. We had no indoor plumbing. Neither did my grandparents at that time.

My papaw was a farmer. He and my grandmother raised their own vegetables. They kept chickens and hogs. I remember hog killings at the time of the first December snow, and I was glad my papaw thought me too young to be of any help during the process. My family moved from the farm to a little better rental house at Sitka when I was almost six where my mother began preparing me to go to school by telling me how much she enjoyed her education in the one-room school she attended. With her teacher's encouragement she had repeated the eighth grade so that she could learn as much as she could since her mother would not allow her to board with a family near Flat Gap High School in order to continue her education.

Mine was the first generation in the mountains *not* to attend one-room schools, but their spirit survived in 1959 at Flat Gap School. Some of my classrooms in fact were in wooden buildings with oiled floors. We would drop our pencils through the cracks in order to be excused from class for a few minutes to go under the floor to retrieve them. Pot-bellied stoves in the center of the room provided heat. Lights were incandescent bulbs hanging pendulum fashion from the rafters. These classrooms were like a community of one-room schools located on one campus.

Flat Gap School's main building was a WPA block structure with classrooms surrounding a red-and-white-floored basketball gymnasium. We were the Greyhounds, and our basketball teams

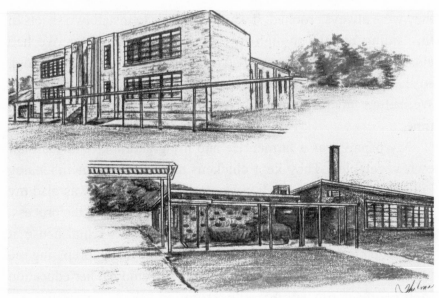

Flat Gap School

were the stuff of mountain legends. My brother swore that it was *my* fault that he ran full speed into one of those old block walls and broke out the better half of a top front tooth. The candy store was in the basement of this building. Here janitors, cooks, and teachers alike would take turns selling us wax bottles of sweet soda, candy cigarettes, or marshmallow-filled Mallo cups. The money was needed for teaching and maintenance supplies.

I first thought about becoming a teacher when I was in the first grade and under the spell of Mrs. Harriet McKenzie, whose path I crossed with dread. Country-school teachers in the mountains of east Kentucky earned reputations that preceded them into the classroom. Mrs. McKenzie presided over the halls of Flat Gap School in Johnson County like a dictator, keeping track of how many times her pupils had gone in the bathroom because too many trips meant trouble. My best friend, Dana Lyons, now a broadcaster on

Paintsville's WSIP radio station, and I would be amazed to find she had kept track of each visit and each circle of *her* hallway. Dana was not in her first-grade class but feared Mrs. McKenzie nonetheless.

Mrs. McKenzie towered over us, wearing a starched Swiss-dotted print dress that looked as if it might have come from a store other than the local Murphy's five and ten where our families had bought our starched, wide-cuffed jeans. Her black-framed glasses did little to hide the eyes of a wise owl. She believed in letting her students see her smile only twice during the school year: the day before the Christmas break (Students would forget they saw her smile by their return) and the last day of school in the spring.

I could recognize and write one letter of the alphabet when I began first grade—the script letter *e*. By the time I left Mrs. McKenzie's class for Mrs. Jewel Ross's second-grade room, I was printing all my letters with carefully instructed penmanship and reading with the students at the blue table reserved for the best readers in the class.

Six years earlier, Mrs. McKenzie had taught my older brother Donald. The story she still told at Bea's Beauty Shop, where she was certain my mother would hear it, was of my brother climbing on top of tables to show off or hiding under tables to look up girls' dresses. Needless to say, he failed the first grade. I believed I would be judged in his likeness. Mrs. McKenzie did me the favor of not judging me by my brother, and in this way taught me my first and most important lesson—to treat each student as an individual.

I remember one morning in particular when I had gone to school not feeling well. Mrs. McKenzie immediately took me aside, spoke to me in the same voice a mother uses to soothe her sick child, and called my father. She *knew* my father. She and her husband Walter had purchased tires from Mountain Tire Service where my father had found work after returning from Dayton. This was the first time I had heard a tender word from Mrs. McKenzie. I had no way of knowing then that I would teach some day, but even so, on that day I learned that Mrs. McKenzie *cared* about me. Recalling her simple act of kindness still reminds me that all my best teachers were *caring* teachers. What I recall most about Flat Gap School was that we were a *community*.

When I look at pictures of groups of students who attended one-room schools, it almost seems as if they were in uniforms, for all the boys are dressed alike in their clean bibbed overalls, and although the girls' dresses are of variously patterned calico, they are styled alike and probably cut from similar mail-order patterns. No one had much cash money, and no one had more than anyone else in the way of material possessions. There was no TV or Internet connection to the outside world to tell them they were poor. Students attended school to learn, and teachers, who were looked up to as community leaders, imprinted the value of education upon them.

Pictures of me in the elementary grades are likewise similar to those of everyone else in my classes. We boys had flattop haircuts and wore white undershirts under our collared print shirts. Our jeans were deep navy blue (if new) with turned-up cuffs so that they would last as long as the knees did not wear through or longer with patches that were not in style but not ridiculed. Our shoes were black and white Converse sneakers. I remember being afraid of falling and muddying or tearing my clothes because I understood money was not easy to come by. Our daddies farmed, mined coal, or worked in town. Our mothers were fifties mothers—homemakers who kept the house spotless, did the Monday wash in Maytag wringer washers on back porches, worked in the garden, sewed our quilts, mended our clothes, and timed the cooking of the nightly cornbread to perfectly coincide with our fathers' arrival home from work.

The sense of community that one-room school teachers encouraged was a reflection of the community which surrounded the school buildings themselves, and that community survived in east Kentucky through the fifties and sixties—my childhood years. My world was not limited to the family unit of my mother, father, brother, and me. It was filled with grandparents, uncles, aunts, cousins, neighbors, and teachers. We knew if we misbehaved, we would be reprimanded by any one of these individuals who made up our community.

Jasper and Monnie Slone, circa 1917.

CHAPTER TWO

I had the luxury of knowing all four of my grandparents. My mother's father, Millard Huff, was a coal miner who, when the mines played out in Van Lear, moved into a boarding house in Holden, West Virginia, near Logan, to continue to do what he loved—mine coal. Mining was a more dangerous occupation in the fifties and sixties than it is today. I carry two dominant images of my grandfather with me today: one of a humble man who quietly spoiled his grandson whenever he could and one of a strong man who did not complain with the pain when his jaw was broken from a slate fall.

My grandfather Huff never drove a car. My father would take him to meet another miner in Pike County who "hauled" men to work. When we would go to the Dairy Queen on Broadway in Paintsville in my father's two-tone brown and cream '56 Chevy, my papaw would ride beside me in the back. Out of respect he got to sit by the window. I can still see him behind the half-rolled-down glass, reaching me a quarter and telling me to "go buy myself a 'comb.'" Although I knew he mispronounced the word *cone*, I never once thought of correcting him, for he was my papaw, and respecting our grandparents was a primary rule in our community. One time when he came home from his three-week stay in West Virginia, I met him on the front porch—his favorite place to chew tobacco and get away from Mamaw's bossing—to see that he had remembered me with a present—a "paddle ball"—a ping pong shaped board with a red rubber ball attached to it with a rubber band. Expensive toys fade from our memories and are replaced by simple loving gifts such as these.

The last years of my papaw Huff's life were spent in and out of the Pikeville Miners' Hospital (today known as the Pikeville Medical Center) dying the slow death of pneumoconiosis—black lung disease. I remember the weight he lost due to the soft food diet he was forced to eat. My mamaw prepared for his breakfast poached eggs and grits—quite a contrast from fresh tenderloin, milk and red-eye gravy, fried potatoes, apples, and eggs he loved to eat for breakfast. While we ate chicken and dumplings prepared from a freshly killed hen, my grandfather would be able to only eat canned soup and bread. I remember visits to the hospital where I could not always ride the elevator (a special treat for a country boy) to my papaw's room because visiting time was restricted for children. I would walk around back of the hospital building to a grassy hill where I could see my papaw standing at the window of his room waving down to me. I suppose I was his favorite grandson, but he loved all children. Not all men relate well to small children, but my papaw was the exception. My mother recalled only one spanking that he gave to any of his three children. It was done to "take her part" in an incident between my mother and her sister Doris who had locked her in a trunk. My papaw could not allow one of his children to be treated this way, so Doris got the whipping she deserved.

My papaw's favorite game was solitaire as he sat upright in his hospital bed, but he would smile and put his cards aside when we visited or when he had the opportunity to talk to the family of the miner in the bed beside him. He missed his work, but most of all he missed his miner buddies. During his lifetime he worked alongside men of various races and religious beliefs. In the face of danger underground, differences didn't matter to him—one of those lessons I *absorbed* when I was growing up in the mountains. My papaw Huff was the first of my four grandparents to die. Our people move in and out of our lives very quickly. We need to take the time to listen to their stories and to absorb their influences, and we ought to be writing these stories down so that they might survive generations longer than those handed down to us through the oral tradition.

Children who grow up without knowing their grandparents lose out on the extra parenting they provide. Mine taught me the value of *hard work* through example. My grandmother Huff carried wash water from the creek when the old dug well went dry in summer. She kept the house spotless, cared for her children, prepared all the meals, as well as did outside work on the farm. She fed and helped butcher hogs, wrung the necks off chickens for Sunday dinner, tended to her own chicken house for eggs, and could outwork many men when it came to planting potatoes or transplanting tobacco.

My father's mother, Monnie Slone, was a little slip of a lady with long hair, that I never saw worn down, and humble, loving eyes that I always saw through glasses, who was busy with work her whole life long. My father told me she played the five-string banjo—drop-thumb style, but that was before I was born. She always had the time for stories if not for music. An undiagnosed diabetic, she had to have a leg amputated to save her life. On one leg she still managed the housework, taking pride in how clean and organized were her kitchen and her home. Farm hands considered her midday cooking a bonus as valuable almost as their pay. They looked forward to her supper-style lunches, a respite from their Blue Bird Vienna sausages and crackers purchased at Alonzo Caudill's country store.

Jasper and Monnie on the porch.

Mamaw loved having company, so that she might hear compliments about her housekeeping. If I could go inside her home today to find her there, she would be seated on the couch outside her wheelchair sewing pieces for a quilt top. These pieced quilt tops she gave away to family and neighbors. The black and white television might be on for noise. If the Porter Wagoner show was on, she would be paying attention, watching and listening to "…the ugliest man I have ever seen, but he can *sing*."

Her husband Jasper was known throughout Johnson and Lawrence counties for his apple crop, but he raised tobacco and strawberries for cash crops as well. He and my grandmother took pride in hosting "farmers' field days" when all the neighboring farmers and their families would gather to share a good meal, win door prizes like electric fans, and learn about the latest farming methods and products from the UK county extension agent. Papaw plowed with horses or mules. He never owned a tractor. He was song leader and an elder in the Old Hood United Baptist church, but could cuss a blue streak as he worked a team behind a plow. I rode the rubber tired spray wagon with him and helped him prune or spray his orchard. He let me drive the sled that carried apple crates and picking bags. I learned "gee" and "haw" to get the horse to turn, but horses never listened to me like they did to Papaw.

My papaw Slone told me many times that he thought I should become a preacher, and I suppose all teachers have a gift for preaching that they rely on in order to reach their students now and then, but as he described the *call* to preach, I never received it. Of all my grandparents my papaw Slone was the one most connected to the land. Farming had been handed down through the generations since his grandfather, John Slone, moved to east Kentucky from Scott County, Virginia, in 1850. John Slone sold the saddle from the horse he rode on to Kentucky in order to buy the 150 acres that today make up my grandfather's old home place on Slone Branch just off Route 201 in Johnson County near the Lawrence County line.

My other three grandparents valued education and saw it as a way to improve lives, but my papaw Slone was afraid that education would lead me from the farm, so he was my only grandparent who did not encourage my education. My mamaw Slone would whisper in my ear for me to follow her in her wheelchair to her bedroom where she would open a bureau drawer and take a twenty-dollar bill, wad it up in her hand, and put her hand inside mine. I was never to let Papaw know she had given me money to help me with my college expenses.

It took me many years to understand my papaw's attitude toward education. Farming was all he knew, and he could not stand the thought of his grandson leaving the land. He defined *work* as physical labor. He was not happy that my father left the farm for a job in town, but at least my father was working with his hands. He respected my father's job. He could not understand the value of an education that would prepare me to teach. My mamaw understood that there might be an easier way of life than farming and, unlike my papaw, wanted me to live my own dream. As she sat in her wheelchair on the floor of Johnson Central's gymnasium and listened to me give the valedictory address, I know she was proud and wanted me to be the first in my family to earn a college degree.

CHAPTER 3

My father and his father had an interesting relationship. I never saw my papaw Slone drive a car or truck, but I heard the story of the only truck he ever owned, so he must have had a license if only for a brief time. He had purchased a truck to transport his apple crop to Paintsville so that he could sell—"peddle"—his apples to the townspeople. My father at age seventeen drove cattle trucks and so was an experienced driver, but he had too much to drink one evening and wrecked, breaking both shoulders in the accident and totaling the truck. My grandfather never forgave my father completely, and my father never forgave my grandfather for having him "turned out of church"—removed from the membership roll of the Hood's Creek United Baptist Church—because of his recklessness. They loved each other until the day my papaw died though. But I do not recall either using the word *love* in relation to one another or to me. I recall acts that in my mind proved that their love for one another was still strong.

My father cut my grandfather's hair on the front porch of my grandparents' home using a pair of hand shears or clippers. I can remember my grandfather seated in a straight-back, cane-bottom chair draped in a towel as my father trimmed his thinning gray hair. In my poem titled "Home Haircuts," I imagine my grandfather cutting my father's hair when he was just a boy in that same ladder-back chair and on that same narrow banistered porch. Then I record my memory of seeing my father return the favor for his father when his father had grown old. I close the poem with: "Father and son go out onto the porch/ To give and receive what has been given and received before."

There is quite a caretaking tradition in the mountains. Families do all they can to prevent sending their loved ones to nursing homes. I recall serving on the University of Kentucky Community College system's promotion and tenure committee with a nursing instructor from Southeast Community College. She and her husband were native eastern Kentuckians. Her husband's mother had suffered a stroke and was hospitalized nearby. Her stay had been a long one, and the time was growing near for her release. All that could be done for her had been done, and the hospital would keep her no longer. The lady died on the very day she was to be released. That was also to be the day that her family would have to place her in a nursing home. The nursing instructor came to our next meeting grieving, but she was so relieved, as was her husband, that God had taken her loved one home before she could be admitted to the nursing home. Mountain families postpone that step as long as possible because they have been taught to become caretakers of their parents when they grow old as a way of returning the love that was freely given to them as children.

The symbol of the relationship between my father and my grandfather is found in the memory I have of watching my father cut my grandfather's hair. To my papaw, a haircut was not a good reason to go to Paintsville. He would take a seat where the cut hair could be swept easily underneath the green-shingled banister and into the front yard. My grandfather was happy to let my father cut his hair. He would fuss at my grandmother's hair cutting but would not complain to my father. I can remember sitting on the wood steps that led up to the porch and thinking to myself that I would always remember this moment. I was nine or ten and had no idea why. I now realize that although he had his disagreements with his father, my father was doing for his father what his father had done for him when he was a boy. We all eventually become the caretakers of our parents that they were for us when we were small. Roles simply reverse. Love is given and received, even if not spoken.

CHAPTER FOUR

I did not look forward to the start of school each fall, for it meant that I would be forced to sit inside. I loved the outdoors and spent most of my time in the woods or in or near the water. I could sit most of the day on creek banks fishing for catfish if the water was muddy or sundads if it was clear. I loved to walk the black pine-lined ridges looking for squirrels, and my swing was a tree swing made with chain not with ropes that hung from a white oak tree 200 yards behind the treeline in the woods behind our home.

I wanted to know what was just over the top of each hill. My father had told me stories about walking these same hills when he was a young man. As he walked, he did not stay on roadbeds that bordered creeks but instead took to the hills to shorten distances between his house and the houses of friends he visited or girls he courted. My papaw Slone would warn me of old dug wells covered with rotting boards. He knew their location because he had roamed these hills and bottoms himself as a boy and had hoed corn on land that during my childhood had been allowed to grow up in briars and sapling trees. He and my father knew the location of every old home place, and even the primary barn on his farm had once been a house. Instead of tearing it down, he just built on stalls for his horses and mules and a storage shed for his spray wagon.

Once the school year started, I was fine. I would still stare longingly out the windows, but my early teachers took care of that quickly and convinced me to stay "on task." I learned very early that I could compete with my classmates and earn praise from my teachers. I was taught to take pride in my class work and to put my studies before my outdoor adventures. In school I saw a way to be successful, and from my mother I had learned that success in school might lead to a better way of life. I saw my father come home at night from his job recapping tires. His back would hurt so badly that after supper he would lie on the living room floor to get some ease. He didn't have the strength left to throw a ball with me. He did not even lift his head to watch the black and white TV. He knew that he must rest for the next day's work and that only *if* he worked, would we have food and a place to live. He did not need to lecture me in order to get me to do my homework. I saw with my own eyes what my life would be like without an education.

Not long after returning to the mountains of east Kentucky to teach, I discovered a nearby writer who, like me, loved nature and wanted to discover what was over the top of each hill, a writer who had watched his parents work in the cotton fields near Lafayette, Alabama, where he had spent his childhood—James Still.

Professional writers abound in east Kentucky. Their proximity to Big Sandy Community and Technical College has been a great benefit to my students and to me. Those teachers who have remained in the mountains for brief periods and have not taken the time to discover the talent here have missed the opportunity to discover and share Kentucky model writers with their students. Sadly, many native east Kentuckians who return to teach in their home area do not encourage their students to read Kentucky writers. They give lip service to valuing their culture, but they somehow feel it is inferior and so choose not to introduce their students to writers who reflect it.

East Kentucky writers constitute the heart of Appalachian literature, which is part of southern literature. Both rest comfortably within American literature. Reading Appalachian literature is especially important for mountain students who share a set of common experiences. Mountain students need to see the value of all literature, but becoming familiar with the literature of their own culture provides affirmation that inspires confidence. Students learn that stories they heard from their grandparents are worth re-telling. Appalachian writers help teach mountain students that they are capable of discovering their own voices through writing.

One such writer who inspires my students was the Alabama native, James Still, who lived some seventy of his ninety-four and a half years in Knott County, Kentucky, which borders the county where Big Sandy Community and Technical College is located. My own education did not include reading Mr. Still's writing. I discovered *River of Earth* through reading a literature research paper in one of the first college Writing II classes I taught. I remember that when I admitted to my student that I had not heard of Mr. Still, she looked at me as if she felt sorry for me. My graduate degree in English had left me unaware of the literature of my own people. So I took the time to read Mr. Still's works: his poems, short stories, his children's stories, and his classic novel *River of Earth.*

James Still's works made me feel as if I'd come home. I had discovered a writer who did everything in his writing that I had been trying to encourage my own students to do. He noticed the small details in nature and the common characteristics shared within all humanity. He wrote about humility, joy, pain, guilt, forgiveness, and the cycle of life, death, and rebirth. He used the language of ordinary speech because he innately knew this was language that would last. I began showing my students his poems from the collection, *The Wolfpen Poems*. They loved them.

Kentucky Educational Television produced a documentary about his life and career. Mr. Still was given the opportunity to read several of his poems at various intervals in the piece. I was reminded of an old record I had used in my high school teaching days. Robert Frost read his own poems. Hearing Frost read, immediately destroyed the mistaken illusion students had about Frost's poems being simple nature poems. By listening to the poet read his own work, we could hear the edge of nature's cruelty that Frost intended for us to hear.

I began to duplicate the poems Still read in the KET documentary. As he sat on an old ladder-back, cane-bottom chair and read from behind his half-frame glasses "White Highways," my students read along. Through listening to Mr. Still read his poem, their attention was drawn to familiar places, and they were encouraged to think about them in a new way. In "White Highways," for example, Mr. Still describes the new four-lane highways like Route 80 between Prestonsburg and Hazard. He illustrates the mastery of engineering required to push back the mountains and ford the rivers. Then he calls the readers' attention to the past that shaped their own culture—to the creek-bed roads their grandparents traveled. In his poem these old twisting roads become symbols for a vanishing way of life when people had the time to get to know each other. They were a part of a Kentucky *community*, the type of community Henry County writer, Wendell Berry, defends today.

Discovering one's own literature has a way of illuminating the writing process. Students begin to see that writers can express universal truths while relating their own experiences. They discover that their grandparents' stories can become the grist for their own writing.

Students also discover while learning about James Still that their only hope to become better writers is to become readers. In the KET documentary, Mr. Still is pictured taking boxes of books to children at the various one-room schools in the county. He loved to get books into the hands of children. He would take one box to a single school, pick up books there that the children had already read, and take them to a different school. His purpose was to instill in the children a love for reading.

Mr. Still's own love for reading is illustrated in the documentary as he talks about his days at Lincoln Memorial University working as a janitor in the library. After "rubbing up" the tables, he would have the whole place to himself. He would read until he fell asleep on piles of magazines. His love for reading inspired him to write. Students likewise must find what they enjoy reading if they expect to write well.

The story of James Still's adopted daughter, Teresa Bradley, came to me through a student of mine who knew her. Carla described Teresa as a wonderful teacher who went out of her way to build a community of learners at Knott County Central High. Carla met with me one day to discuss a topic for her cultural presentation in her Appalachian Studies class. Each semester my students go out into the five-county area the college serves to find a guest to invite on campus or a person to interview on video. They choose topics such as Appalachian art, Bluegrass music, the Old Regular Baptist religion, coal mining in the forties and fifties, and race relations among miners in coal camps. After I show a model videotape of a guest presenting to my class, I take time to meet with students to refine topics. My Knott County student had become interested in James Still.

Mr. Still's funeral had been on May first of the preceding spring, and Carla had the idea of requesting an interview with his adopted daughter, Teresa Bradley. We were both unsure whether she would permit the interview, but when Carla asked her, I'm sure she let her know that in my class we were studying his works, *The Wolfpen Poems* and *River of Earth*, and that I was making young people aware of a legendary Kentucky author who lived and wrote in the neighboring county. In appreciation, Teresa granted the interview, so my student and I met again to prepare a list of questions we wanted to ask.

Teresa provided my students with an unforgettable interview. Seated on Mr. Still's bed, she told us about his reading habits. He read three hours a day, and his town home and log home were filled with thousands of books. She described his writing. He wrote with a pen and seldom made errors. His writing was very succinct. He would sometimes make editorial comments in the margins but not often. She said that watching him write was like watching a potter or a glass blower. He never used a computer. Mrs. Mary C. Bingham, whose family owned the *Louisville Courier Journal*, gave him a word processor, and he would often say, "You need to teach me how to use it." But when the time came, and his daughter said, "Let's go," he always found an excuse not to begin. "He didn't like change," Teresa said.

She said his bed contained stacks and stacks of letters from his readers and from fellow writers. She said he had kept all his correspondence from writers he knew. Fellow Knott County residents would have no idea—writers such as Robert Frost, Harriet Simpson Arnow, Margaret Mitchell, and on and on. Teresa had met Ms. Arnow when she had come to Hindman to visit Mr. Still. She described her tiny glasses, duster, and sensible shoes. "She looked like your granny." The job of deciding where this correspondence should be archived had fallen upon her, and she was in the process of sorting it all and making the necessary decisions.

Teresa often slipped and spoke of Mr. Still in the present tense. Once she even caught herself doing so, corrected herself, and asked her audience to forgive her. She was so accustomed to his presence—his voice. At that point she spoke of the things she missed about the man: He had *kind eyes*. You could see in those eyes that he was not pretentious. His *hands* made him the man he was. They were strong from his love of the outdoors and gardening, but still gentle enough to hold the hand of a child.

Teresa went on to tell my class about Mr. Still's childhood. She referred to the poem that was published on page one of the *Lexington Herald* on May 1, 2001, the day of Mr. Still's funeral, entitled "Those I Want in Heaven With Me Should There Be Such a Place." She explained each reference to his childhood including "Aunt" Fanny who diapered and comforted him when he was a toddler. Fanny was not related, as Mr. Still's use of quotes would indicate, but was instead a beloved African American lady who was his nanny. Teresa said Mr. Still never stopped writing. Even in sickness during his last days in the hospital, he was working on a manuscript— a story about his childhood.

Through the Teresa Bradley interview, my students had the opportunity to learn about Mr. Still's connection to his adopted place— the hills of east Kentucky. Near the interview's close, Carla, my student, gave Teresa a copy of my collection of poems, telling her that his writing had inspired my own, and asked if there were anything she would like to add. I will always remember the introduction to her reply: "Well, just this…"

She said that something happened on the day of his funeral. She said that she believed in signs or "coincidences." She went to Mr.

Still's home to get some things that needed to be "where *he* was": his glasses, his straw hat, etc. When she entered his home, she left the door open. While she was going through his things, she looked up in surprise to see a tailless squirrel standing in the room. The squirrel hopped up on a table on which the manuscript pages of *From the Mountain From the Valley*, Mr. Still's last collection of poems, had been placed. The squirrel caused a single poem to fall to the floor. Teresa picked it up to read its title, "The Bright Road," a poem about the path to Heaven. The squirrel then ran over and buried itself in a pair of Mr. Still's socks. She said when the squirrel decided to leave, that it walked toward the door and stood and looked up at her as if to say, "I've done what I came to do." There were two cats in the home. "What was the chance," she said, "of a squirrel getting into a house with those two big cats inside?" In an interview James Still granted to L. Elisabeth Beattie for the book *Conversations With Kentucky Writers*, Mr. Still, when asked about his early reading habits and education, told the same story his daughter related to my class about his first grade teacher. She was the best teacher he ever had because she was a "hands-on" teacher. On the first day of class she wrote his name on a sheet of paper on his desk and handed him an ear of corn to shell. He was to use grains of corn to outline his name. By the end of the day he knew how to spell and write his own name. She also taught them to "grow things." Planting and gardening would become his lifelong love. She let them perform stories and poems as plays: "We acted out. I recall *Hiawatha*. We acted *Hiawatha*. I remember I was a *squirrel*."

Many of my students understood because they felt they had received their own spiritual signs about lost loved ones and were reminded of the spiritual signs in my poem, "Feather Crowns." She had been sent a spiritual sign to comfort her, telling her that her father was in a better place; she need not worry about him.

James Still died on April 28th of 2001. He was interviewed for my class in late November, 2000. He was ninety-four and a half years old. When asked, "Do you have a favorite piece that you have written?" Mr. Still responded that *River of Earth* stood out as one of his favorites. He was very proud that some forty-five colleges across the nation had adopted the novel for use in literature classes. He was grateful, for he said school adoptions "keep books alive." He also spoke with pride about his soon-to-be-released University Press of Kentucky published collection of poems, *From the Mountain— From the Valley*.

As my students listen to this, Mr.Still's last interview, they become interested in the process of creative writing. When Mr. Still was asked about the creative process, he said that writing "comes from your head" and that nobody had ever really explained the creative process. Students familiar with *River of Earth* note the strength of the mother Alpha. When asked about the role of women in traditional mountain culture, he said that women run the world; men just haven't found it out yet. He recalled when he taught at Morehead State University, women faculty were not paid the same as men faculty: "I want them paid the same as men for the same jobs."

When Mr. Still was asked about changes he had noticed in young people and in education in general, he spoke with greatest determination. He recalled presenting at a meeting of retired teachers. He knew most of them. He said as he looked around the room, he knew why Johnny couldn't read. It was because the *teachers* didn't read. They did not keep up. They completed college, received a degree, and thought their reading and education ended at this point. He said his own education was directly related to the independent reading he did while he was in college. He said teachers should be motivators and that college "just opens the doors." That door must remain open throughout one's life, and that open door is most important for *teachers* who should inspire students to read throughout their lives.

In his often quoted poem "Heritage," James Still writes and closes his poem with, "Being of these hills/ Being one with the fox stealing into the shadows/ One with the newborn foal/ The lumbering ox drawing green beech logs to mill/ One with the destined feet of man climbing and descending/And one with death rising to bloom again/ I cannot go/ Being of these hills I cannot pass beyond." He could not have better expressed his closeness to the natural world around him than in these words and in the words of another poem he talked about during the course of the interview.

In evidence that Mr. Still truly was "one with the fox stealing into the shadows," he talked about writing the poem titled "Death of a Fox." He had been driving down around London, Kentucky, late one foggy night when all of a sudden, out of the blackness a dog appeared in the middle of the road. He did all he could to avoid hitting it but could not. He was sure the dog was killed instantly. The next day he sat down at his table to draft a letter, but instead wrote the poem, "Death of a Fox." The poem was true except he replaced the dog with a fox. Perhaps he was unsure on the morning after as to whether the animal might have really been a fox. In the poem he asks whether forgiveness can be found anywhere. He asks for forgiveness from God, but he doubts it will be given.

This simple poem touches on the human condition. We all feel guilt and at one time or another have sought forgiveness for our mistakes. Everyone has his or her own story about carrying guilt. Mine involved the killing of an animal too. When I was sixteen, I had a 1960 four-door Ford Falcon. I loved to wash it, shine the baby moon hubcaps and park it in my grandparents' front yard so that all who drove by their home on Route 201 could see it. One afternoon when my grandparents were inside the house, I started the car, and as I began to move forward, I felt one thud and then another and immediately realized what I had done. I had run over Daisy, my grandmother's dog. I suppose she was injured so badly that she dragged herself off to the hills and died there, for we never saw the dog again. I never told my grandmother what had happened to the dog. I had even convinced myself that Daisy might return some day. That hope was in vain, for my grandmother went to her grave without me ever telling her the truth about what happened to the dog. I carry that guilt with me today just as Coleridge's ancient mariner wore the albatross around his neck and was cursed with having to tell his story over and over to strangers. See—I have yet again told the story that is my own curse of guilt. I hope Mr. Still felt better after writing "Death of a Fox," but I suspect he did not and continued to feel the guilt that I also still feel even after sharing my own story. James Still did us all a kindness by speaking to the human condition from which none of us can escape.

Mr. Still was always doing acts of kindness for his readers and for young people in particular. One of his final acts of kindness was this special interview done especially for Big Sandy Community and Technical College students.

As Mr. Still was talking to my class about the thousands of books in his town home and in the old Amburgy log house, he explained how excited he was to have discovered still another Appalachian writer. He had just read the memoir *Creeker* by Linda Scott DeRosier. With excitement in his voice, he described the book and recommended it to my students. I remember his words: "Only a woman could have written that book." Linda Scott DeRosier is a native of my home county—Johnson. She and I first met at the Kentucky

Book Fair in Frankfort where we were seated across from one another signing our books. She told me that she would be teaching at Pikeville College in the spring and would love to speak to my Appalachian literature class on the Pikeville campus of Big Sandy Community and Technical College.

She gave the lecture she promised to my class on our Pikeville campus in the 2002 spring semester. As I introduced her to my students, I played the tape of Mr. Still's interview so that she could hear him say that he had read and enjoyed her book. She was thrilled and humbled. Linda was writer-in-residence that semester at her alma mater, Pikeville College, where she was teaching a writing course. To hear her speak about her writing was to hear the story of a writer who has been *forced* to publish in juried periodicals in order to obtain ratings and promotions and maintain tenure. Through the encouragement of a friend of hers and the grandmother of one of my students, Gwen Holbrook, she spent one summer writing the story of a shy mountain girl who discovered her place after years of travel, degrees, and college teaching positions.

College students had the chance to hear a success story from someone who talked just like their parents or grandparents. "There is something I tell all my audiences when I speak about *Creeker* and about my own writing: You really ought to be writing! You ought to be getting your stories down on paper. It takes about two generations for family stories to seem significant. If you don't think getting these stories down is important, ask your mother if she wishes she had written down the stories her grandmother told *her*."

One of Linda's degrees was earned from Harvard University. During an early phone call to campus to inquire about housing in the Cambridge area, a secretary, as she was reading off an address, spelled out H-a-r-v-a-r-d as if, from Linda's east Kentucky accent, she had decided that Linda must be illiterate. Students in the mountains enjoy hearing stories like Linda's because they desperately want to be proud of their culture and of their older relatives who reflect that culture through their speech. At the same time they are painfully aware that their way of speaking can be the target of ridicule in other places— even in other parts of their own state.

Ms. DeRosier told my students the story of receiving an honorary degree from Pikeville College. She explained that friends were in attendance from all over the state and country who had known her over the years. At that moment she realized that she was glad she had told the *truth*—that she had been *herself* everywhere she had been. She explained that telling the truth was the secret of her success in her own writing. For example, she said as she wrote *Creeker*, she first used all the real names for the people involved in her life. That's where the *energy* was. Then later she went back and changed those names that she felt she needed to change because she had written something negative, and she did not want to hurt their feelings. Staying with the real names while allowing the first draft to *flow* helped her by giving her writing the energy that comes with writing the truth.

We asked Linda about her excellent memory for details. She gave a beautiful response: Writing is a self-generating process. One memory triggers another, and so it goes. She might never have recalled some of the details such as her boyfriend's yellow Banlon sweater had she not first thought about and written about the house fire in which the sweater was destroyed. Yes, Mr. Still, we may not be able to describe the creative process, but we can teach students that writing is a tool that evokes memory, and that memories like your own of the nanny who diapered you and the ginger pony that took you on your first adventures and your dog Jack, "your boon companion," are the raw material for writing that captures moments in time, once thought forgotten.

In an interview for Kentucky Educational Television, Linda was asked the question, "Where do you think your book will be years from now on the shelf with other Kentucky books?" Her response was that she hoped students in rural counties in Kentucky like our home county of Johnson could read it. She hoped that it could serve as an affirmation of their own culture, a culture that is different and separate from the culture of young people who grow up in towns. She hoped that by reading her story, young people might see the *truth* about both her successes and failures so that they might know it is ok to make their own mistakes and to learn from them.

I like the fact that Linda's story is also that of a *teacher*. After all she has spent her life teaching, and beneath the surface of her memoir, she is teaching young people to set goals and take pride in achieving them.

I teach a college writing class at the high school where Johnson County students, who would have gone to Linda's old high school, Meade Memorial, now attend. Caleb Branham, her best friend Gwen's grandson, was in my class. He was proud that he was mentioned in the book, even if not by name, playing on the front porch of his grandmother's cabin. Four rural high schools consolidated in 1968 to form Johnson Central High School. Students who live within the city limits of Paintsville still attend the city school, Paintsville High, the school where Linda heard the cheerleaders recite the cheer, "Two bits, four bits, six bits, a dollar, send those Creekers back up the holler," the source of her title.

I read for my students the passage from *Creeker* in which the author describes country stores. She calls the aroma in those stores "country store perfume." Even though my students are only seventeen or eighteen, they have heard their parents' stories from memories of those who operated these country stores.

When I was a high school student in Johnson County, I thought everyone who wrote books came from somewhere else. I read Jesse Stuart's short stories, but he was from Greenup County, northwest of Ashland, and that area was the big city to those of us south of Louisa. There is a quiet affirmation that occurs when students see that writers like Linda Scott DeRosier and James Still have become successful by writing about their own culture. Students feel *their* people are of value and that they themselves might have something worthwhile to write about.

CHAPTER FIVE

My mother was born in Van Lear, Kentucky, but the family soon moved near Hood's Creek to live alongside my grandmother's parents on her home place in a log house with two front entrances. This old log house shaped my mother's self-image as a child. In the late thirties and early forties country homes were being built as wood

Joene Huff Slone, 1944.

frame structures with wood siding exteriors. Log houses were being remodeled to resemble newer homes with the addition of modern kitchens and baths and exterior painted siding to cover the old square-cut logs. My mother was ashamed of the old square-cut log house. Even after it was torn down and replaced with a modern home, she would not show me pictures of the log house she grew up in. While spending the night with my grandmother though, I did find a photo of the home. It was beautiful! It was the kind of log home we dream about today. It had a long front porch that connected the two living areas much like the duplexes of today. Instead of being built close to the highway as its replacement was, it was built to nestle perfectly in the hollow between two hills and high on a natural plateau far away from potential flooding of the creek. My mother should have been proud of the home, but children can be cruel to one another and out of ignorance thought my mother's family backward for not keeping up with modern styles. My mother allowed others to make her feel ashamed. Regardless of their circumstances, students should never allow others to make them feel ashamed. My best teachers were perfectly comfortable with their roots and encouraged their students to be likewise. They treated us as equals regardless of how much money our fathers made or whether our families' homes were made of logs.

One east Kentucky writer who taught her readers not to be ashamed and instilled pride into all who read her work was Knott County's Verna Mae Slone. My classroom door is always open to writers and their stories. The seed for using model writers was sown while I taught high school in Gallatin County in northern Kentucky. The local public library received a grant to fund a guest writer program for the county schools. A Viet Nam War poet was hired to read his works to classes and to talk to the students about writing. As the poet read and spoke about his writing, I recall students' faces lit up, showing more of an interest in writing than I had ever seen before. There was just something special about a *writer* talking about writing. He discussed his influence, the World War I poetry of Wilfred Owen. I had assigned Owen poems before, but I had never before seen such student interest. Here was a writer who wrote from his own experiences, wartime experiences form the not-so-distant past. The year was 1979. Students remembered seeing video of the Viet

Nam War on TV as children. They remembered hearing their parents discussing the war, and some had fathers or uncles who had fought in it. I learned that students learn how to write by listening to writers.

Not long ago I was excited to discover that writer Verna Mae Slone's great granddaughter was enrolled in my Appalachian literature class. I soon discovered that she and her "granny" were close. She would bring in recent photos of Mrs. Slone, photos that had been taken during a weekend visit to her home. After class one day she told me that this semester was to be her last at Big Sandy Community and Technical College and that she had wanted to take the class in which her great grandmother's book, *What My Heart Wants to Tell*, was discussed before transferring from our college. She was justifiably proud of her "granny" and her writing.

Mrs. Slone is a true Appalachian storyteller. *What My Heart Wants To Tell* is really a series of *stories* passed down through her father to her. She says her father would have been a stand-up comedian if he had lived in today's time, for he was always telling stories. He would tell them while the family worked in the fields or while he worked making chairs for Mrs. Lloyd at Alice Lloyd College.

Mrs. Slone's writing is filled with richness of detail. Even when she *speaks*, students can tell that she is a writer. She describes the logs in her grandmother's cabin for example by saying that she likes to think that they heard her mother's cry when she was born or maybe heard her grandfather whisper his marriage proposal to her grandmother. My students often tell me that they take *What My Heart Wants To Tell* home to read only to find a family member has borrowed it.

During the last four weeks of each semester's class, my students invite guests to talk about their art, writing, occupation, or past set of experiences related to the mountain culture, and each semester we usually have the opportunity to meet at least one or two writers, either in person or through a video recording. Mrs. Slone was almost eighty-nine, and her health prevented her from presenting to my students in person, but her great granddaughter Shea agreed to do a taped interview with her. Interviews such as these become keepsakes for students, worth much more than the grade assigned. I duplicated the tape for Shea so that she has two copies to keep in separate safe places—a lasting memory of her "granny" she can keep forever much as she will forever hold onto the dolls and quilts Mrs. Slone has lovingly sewn for her. Prior to the interview, Shea and I discussed questions she could ask. Through experience I know which questions will inspire answers and illustrations that might help students learn about writing.

Mrs. Slone began by asking about our class, and when she learned my last name, of course asked whether she and I were related. When the answer was no, she then wanted to know how I spelled my last name. She remembered the former mayor of Louisville, Harvey Sloane, who, when he was running for governor, had asked for her vote. Her reply was, "When you take that *a* out of your name, I will vote for you." One of Mrs. Slone's most admirable qualities is her humble sincerity. She knew of Slones who had *changed* the spelling of their last name when they had moved away from the mountains. "It's their right to change the spelling, but it is my right to resent it."

From there Mrs. Slone went on to explain why she had written the book, *What My Heart Wants to Tell*. She believed "God had a hand in it." She had grown tired of the lies and half-truths told about the mountain people and wanted to get the record straight. She called much of what had been written about mountain people *degrading*. Her original purpose was to communicate the truth to her grandchildren, so she just had enough copies printed so they could each have a copy. One of her grandchildren's English teachers read the stapled book, which at that time was titled *In Remembrance*, and liked it. Mrs. Slone thought, "If an English teacher likes it, maybe it *is* good." A professor at Alice Lloyd College heard about the book and sent a segment to the *Louisville Courier Journal*. After it was published, she received a call from National Public Radio and was asked if the segment could be read on the air. Her reply was, "Only if you get someone from the mountains to read it. I don't want it ruined by a reader with a northern accent." How inspiring it is for my students to hear the pride in her voice! A region's dialect should in no way inspire degradation. To hear Mrs. Slone say she is proud of our way of talking affirms what my students have wanted to feel about the dialect of their grandparents for a long, long time—*cultural pride*.

When asked how old she was when she began writing, Mrs. Slone replied that she was sixty-five. Non-traditional college students, who often feel that they are too old to be starting college, love to hear that one is never too old to pursue his or her dream.

Shea next asked her about her reading habits. Shea and I had thought to ask this question by remembering Mr. Still's response about his own reading habits and his strong feelings about the importance especially for teachers to continue reading. She said she still read three books a week, subscribed to four magazines, and belonged to a book club. Students who have recently read nothing more than their assigned readings lower their heads in embarrassment after hearing this.

Four generations were together in Mrs. Slone's son's home for the interview. From behind the camera, Shea's mother asked her grandmother to read a poem she had written. My students listened

51

in disbelief as she did not read but instead *recited* the poem she had written and published about abortion. She *spoke* to an audience of young people she hoped would reconsider their beliefs. Her poem expressed *her* belief that the unborn child, in the eyes of God, deserves the opportunity to live. Near the poem's conclusion, Mrs. Slone describes the empty place in the family graveyard where the child—grown into adulthood would have lain. In Heaven she says mother and child will be reunited, and the mother who aborts "will have a great debt to pay."

James Still in the last interview he gave before he died had spoken about his admiration for Verna Mae Slone and her book, *What My Heart Wants To Tell*. He said he liked the idea of someone with limited education writing what was in her heart. I knew from speaking with Mrs. Slone in 1987, that she was also an admirer of Mr. Still's writing and had asked Mr. Still for advice when she first began to publish. Shea asked about her friendship with Mr. Still. Mrs. Slone mentioned one of his last poems with the title, "Those I Want in Heaven With Me Should There Be Such a Place." She loved the poem but had been so upset at Mr. Still because of his word choice in the title that she had written a note on the birthday card she sent him expressing her disappointment. The title implied he might *not* believe in Heaven. Mr. Still later spoke to her and explained that he *did* believe in Heaven. She said she would meet him in Heaven some day, and when she did, she would say to him, "See I *told* you there was such a place!"

Mrs. Slone was proud that Mr. Still and she were often mentioned together in reviews. "We *were* together. We were in the same community writing about the same themes and people." She laughed to think she might have given her audience the impression that they could have been a couple: "We were together in our writing and nothing more." Finding that her words could be misinterpreted, she was laughing at herself. "My father always said, 'Don't ever laugh at anybody, and don't let them laugh at you; laugh *with* them.'" I remind my students that this advice informs her writing. She wrote to stop the laughter of derision. Through her writing she is saying, "Laugh *with* me—not *at* me and my people."

Mrs. Slone volunteered to her great granddaughter that throughout her life she had been thankful for three things: God had provided for us all a way to redemption. He had given her something and had taken something away. God had given her a sense of humor that had sustained her all her life, and He had taken away her love of money. Students reflect upon what they have been *given* and what needs to be *taken away*.

All through the interview, Mrs. Slone is seated in a comfortable rocking chair holding a doll she has been sewing. Her newest dolls are made from men's socks. She no longer sells her dolls because she says she has enough great grandchildren now and can *give* them all away.

Verna Mae Slone's is a native east Kentucky voice arguing for changed perceptions of mountain people. She says of her writing: "It was a miracle; it was just God's plan." If my mother could have read Mrs. Slone's work, she would have never again been ashamed of the log home she grew up in.

CHAPTER SIX

My mother's early lack of self-confidence probably explains why she disliked going to church. Rural churches in the mountains with memberships of fifty or fewer were often provincial—dominated by one extended family. I remember when I was ten, my mother sent me to Easter Sunday service with neighbors. I had gone before with neighbors to revivals. My mother must have felt guilty for only taking me to church herself for funeral services. This particular Sunday would help shape my character in a way my mother never dreamed of. I remember sitting on the hard wooden pew and seeing all the pretty new shoes and clothes, and I remember we children outnumbered adults. As brown paper bags of Easter candy were passed around to all the children, I remember *how* the candy was given to me. The pretty lady who gave it to me looked at me with derision. Her eyes said, "You only came for the candy. You are not welcome here." I did not try to explain what I had felt to my mother. I knew she would feel bad for having sent me. As I grew older, I realized she would have understood, for she *herself* remembered attending a church where she was made to feel inferior to those long-standing members who considered the church their own. She bristled at the idea that one had to be on the membership roll in order to enter the gates of Heaven, and she did not believe membership guaranteed admission. Hers was a quiet, personal faith in God that she practiced at home with her children. She read the Bible to me at night and taught me the importance of faith and silent prayer. She did not believe one need practice his or her faith inside a particular denomination's churchhouse in order to receive spirituality. She taught me about spiritual signs like the feather crown—a crown of feathers flowing clockwise that forms in the feather ticking of the death-bed pillow—a sign that a loved one had gone to Heaven.

My mother taught my family one last spiritual lesson before she died at age sixty-one. She baby-sat for my son Stephen from the time he was two and a half until he was old enough for school while my wife and I taught. Since she did not learn to drive, my father would bring her to our home each morning. My wife and I felt at ease that our son was in the best of care. When our daughter Beth was born in November 1988, we looked forward to my mother again coming to care for her while we worked.

One December morning Mom came through the door carrying hot gravy and biscuits in one hand and a Christmas gift for our one-month-old daughter in the other. The gift was a doll named Special Blessings. She had my mother's wild black hair. She wore a comfortable waistless housedress and comfortable flat-soled shoes. Her hands were folded (Velcroed really) together in prayer—hence her name. My wife and I did not understand why my mother would purchase a doll designed for an eight-year-old girl—an inappropriate gift for an infant. Beth was not ready for such a grown-up doll. All she could do was lie in the floor and look at the doll. Without being told to, Beth has carried that doll with her wherever she goes. It has traveled to restaurants, ballgames, and shopping malls. It even sat through surgery with her.

Today Beth is sixteen, and Special Blessings is still with her—a part of our family. I have given the doll and my daughter good

Elmo, Donald, and Joene; young Slone family / I am held by Mom, 1954.

night kisses every night for sixteen years. She makes Special Blessings comfortable on the couch in front of the living room window. The only places her doll cannot go are school, the grocery store, and other places where peers might see her and make fun of a girl her age who still carries her doll. She knows her friends would not understand.

Late one evening my mother suffered a heart attack and quietly fell on her side on the couch in her living room. Special Blessings lies on the couch today in our living room while my daughter is in high school, but when she returns home from academic practice in the afternoon, the doll is wherever *she* is.

My mother must have known somewhere deep inside that she would not be with Beth, so she bought her that grown-up doll to stay after she passed. Today, Beth has no memories of her grandmother other than the stories we have told her. She received many dolls during her childhood, but none could ever take the place of Special Blessings.

After my mother's death, I published a poem titled "Reincarnation." Its subject is not reincarnation as it is usually interpreted. In the poem I use the metaphor of a wheel to symbolize the fact that when a loved one dies, a part of that person lives on in the lives of friends and family whose lives she or he has touched. In the poem, my mother lives again to hear the cries of my baby daughter:

Cries of newborn baby girl,
New life in an old mountain home,
A new spoke on an old wheel,
Joined at the hub,
Never traveling any farther than rusty rim.
Two souls softly weep
Soon to be one in spirit lifting and descending.

She knows somewhere inside
That her life is nearly over
Yet just beginning.

Soft death settles on a mountain home.

All swear they hear
Mammaw's voice in baby's cries.
See soul reborn,
A gift to all who know to receive,
A new spoke in the old wheel,
Joined at the soul,
Never traveling farther
Than the rim.

My daughter Beth was born on November 27, 1988. My mother died on February 27, 1989, three months to the date of Beth's birth.

When my mother did not get along at all with the baby, no one could understand. She had always had a way with the elderly and with babies. When Beth and she were together, Beth constantly screamed, and my mother looked as if she wanted to do the same, would age permit. My mother's health was declining. I'm sure she sensed that her life was about to end.

After my mother's death something changed inside our daughter. My mother's spirit seemed to enter our baby girl. Even now those who knew my mother see her spirit in Beth. Beth is like my mother in every conceivable way.

When I read about the reincarnation of my mother's spirit, I have learned to look around the room for an expression on the faces of students who truly understand because they have witnessed the same sort of reincarnation within their own families. One student named Heather was crying as I read the poem and did not even wait until after class to tell me why. Her little brother Cody was born just before his grandfather died. After the grandfather's death Cody began taking on the grandfather's personality traits and habits. He even preferred the same type of clothing as his papaw—bibbed overalls.

One day Cody looked toward Heaven and spoke to his papaw, calling him by a nickname that he had never been told. Cody had the same mannerisms; he liked the same things; he even knew the brand of cigarettes his papaw smoked! Heather wrote a beautiful narrative about the supernatural connection. Her peers listened with respect as they had when hearing my poem.

Students today are open to faith in the unexplainable. They may not be able to personally relate, but they show respect and are not quick to form judgments. My daughter and Cody are each connected to the spirit of someone who loved them but did not live long enough to demonstrate their love.

CHAPTER SEVEN

Spirituality enters teaching whether or not the latest federal court decision is tolerant. Sometimes it is present in the classroom before the teacher is aware. A colleague of mine, Dr. Marie Parsons, had an interest in death crowns or feather crowns. She invited Delmas Saunders, who had preserved his father's feather crown, to bring it to her office so that she could photograph it.

The semester was coming to a close, but most faculty were still on campus averaging final grades. I heard voices in the office suite and stepped outside to see a gray-haired man holding a glass-enclosed feather crown. He was carrying it delicately as if he was afraid of dropping a precious jewel. Under the glass dome resting on polished wood was the feather crown of his father. It had been discovered in his father's deathbed pillow days after he had died.

I remembered that when I was six or seven, my mother had told me about a similar crown that she had known about in the Hood's Creek community of Johnson County where she lived during her late childhood and teen years. She said everyone on the creek believed the crown was a sign to the woman's loved ones that she had gone on to her reward in Heaven. In those days in the mountains of east Kentucky, everyone knew one another and helped one another in a close community. It was widely known that the lady whose feather crown was discovered had lived a Christian life. She had always helped others in times of sickness or need. No one doubted the existence of the crown or the reason for its formation.

I remembered that when my mother told me the story of the feather crown, I formed my own image of a fairy tale princess's crown made of jewels. I could not imagine a crown made of feathers from the stuffing of a pillow, but I did not doubt my mother's story. I carried my belief in the existence of the crown into adulthood but never thought of it again until seeing Mr. Saunders' father's crown. The crown was made of feathers from the ticking inside his father's pillow. Their color was purest white. They were all tightly interwoven—all flowing in the same clockwise direction, forming a small yarmulke-like cap just large enough to cover the crown of the head.

My colleague and I stood there, believers in feather crowns. Marie had twin baby brothers who had died in infancy. A crown of feathers was discovered for each of the babies. Mr. Saunders' father's crown had been discovered in 1958 and had remained a family treasure. It was the only feather crown Mr. Saunders had known of, so when I told him of my belief that the crown was a spiritual sign, he was pleased, though he assured us that his father was not perfect. He said he had considered donating the crown to a museum or to the Mountain Arts Center in Prestonsburg but felt it should remain in his family. He would pass the crown down to his daughter.

Because of my mother's story about a feather crown, I listened and believed. Others present in the office suite had not heard of these crowns and did not believe. They said the crown had formed for some rational, scientific reason. The person dying may have turned his head back and forth so often that the crown was formed. The heat from the head must have also con-

feather crown

tributed to its formation. They could not accept the possibility of miracles. I believed in the crown just as I believed in prayer. After all, both were explained to me as a child when I had no need to suspend belief and faith in things that could not be empirically proven.

Up to this point in my teaching career, I had not *written* anything. I had been too busy teaching, attending graduate school, and jumping through hoops to earn tenure and promotions in the University of Kentucky Community College system. I felt compelled to write a poem about the crown. Three weeks after the end of that spring semester, I began writing my poem "Feather Crowns." That poem has informed my teaching and writing more than any I have ever written or ever will write again. It was the poem I first read to Elderhostel groups visiting Jenny Wiley State Park and east Kentucky for the first time. I read "Feather Crowns" with a pride that comes from a poem that seemed to *need* to be written. I shared the pictures of Mr. Saunders' father's crown. Some believe, and a few have seen a crown themselves:

> *"Feather crowns are real—not imagined," she says to her child,*
> *"A sign from God — sent to show loved ones the certainty of Eden.*
> *You don't need to see to believe that they are real;*
> *Just believe in them and their meaning.*

They are formed in the feather ticking inside the pillowcase;
After death, they may be discovered as lumps in the death bed pillow."
"Have you ever really seen one, Mommy? "
Sixty-one years she lived— believing in them and their meaning—
never seeing.

The child carried his mother's description of the crown into adulthood,
Knowing they were real, but never seeing.
Then, into the college professor's office suite he stately walked,
Delicately carrying the feather crown of his father.

Found in 1958 after the father's death,
Preserved as a family treasure under glass and resting on polished oak,
Shining white as Angel wings, its feathers flowing in clockwise
concentricy,
So tightly woven, forming the shape of the crown of the head.

"I could donate it to a gallery or to the Mountain Arts Center,
But I have a granddaughter, a graduate student at Vanderbilt.
I am eighty-four; the crown will be hers soon.
She will want science to explain."

"Feather crowns are rare you know;
Many never see."
She will hold in hands, but she may not believe,
"A sign from God— sent to show loved ones the certainty of Eden."

These days students and other audiences who listen to the poem
want to believe whether they were raised in any particular religious
denomination or not. We all have a need to know that this world is
not the end.

Upon hearing the poem, a student of mine, Karri Brooks, stayed after class to tell me the story of her own personal spiritual sign. She had waited to tell me alone in fear that strangers might not understand. Those who have lost close loved ones often tell me they have no crown, but they are certain that their loved one is on the other side and OK. Often they feel the presence of the loved one and sometimes call that person one of their guardian angels.

In Karri's case her angels were real. On April 30th of 1999, her best friend since kindergarten was tragically killed in an automobile accident only one month and one week before her upcoming wedding. Karri always believed because of her friend's gentle kindness that if anyone went to Heaven, surely her friend would be there.

Two years after her friend's death, Karri was baptized. Since the two friends had been so close, Karri invited the deceased girl's parents to her baptism. A picture was taken with Karri and her friend's parents. When the pictures were developed, she noticed a perfect circle almost like a bubble directly above her head. Inside the circle was an angel! In the accident her friend had been primarily injured on the left side of her body. The angel was leaning at a slant to the right as if she could not put weight on the left side of her body. Karri was sure the angel was her friend there with her for the service. Her appearance in the photo was Karri's feather crown—her spiritual *sign* that her friend had gone to Heaven.

Karri gave a print of the photo to her dead friend's parents. She thought they too might see the angel and that it might be a comfort to them. To her surprise her friend's parents were expecting the photo. A friend had told them both that as Karri had walked down the aisle in the church to turn her life over to Christ, two angels had appeared over Karri's head. She said that Karri did not walk to the altar; her angels carried her there. Karri's father died when she was seven.

She believes both he and her best friend were with her in church that day. Karri showed me the picture. I was pleased that my poem had caused her to share such a personal story.

Even students who are without faith hear my poem and stories like Karri's and realize the importance of being open to inspiration that might inspire creativity. They understand that the poem, "Feather Crowns," took shape due to the absorbing/listening that I did as a child even though I did not write the poem until my adult teaching years. They learn to observe life a little more closely so that they might not miss their own revelations some day, whether they ever write about them or not. Regardless, I remain forever thankful for the story my mother shared and its confirmation *given* to me later in my life.

CHAPTER EIGHT

Over the past thirty years most of my students have shared the belief that they have nothing to write about. It *is* true that my junior and senior high school students had fewer experiences to draw from than my current non-traditional college students, but all students have experience-based stories to tell.

One summer, I volunteered to teach a writing workshop for a group of underprivileged children. A former student of mine, Debbie Alsip, had e-mailed me, explaining that she was in charge of a summer "camp" for the children of residents of the Paintsville Housing Authority, a low-income housing complex on Sixth Street in my hometown. Like their big city counterparts, Paintsville's public housing projects had their share of problems: drug and alcohol abuse along with their attendant child neglect and abuse as well as addiction-related crime. Debbie said the theme was to be "Awareness of Appalachian Heritage." Outings were planned, such as a visit to The Mountain Homeplace—a local historical re-creation of a mountain village set in 1850. Debbie had been a student of mine in my Appalachian Studies class at the college. She was calling on me to teach the young people about their mountain culture and heritage.

I decided to start off their summer camp with a writing workshop. I walked into the resource center apartment. The dining area had been converted to an office, and a wall had been taken down from between two bedrooms creating a long meeting room. I stood at the end of a series of three tables placed end to end, read a few poems to the children from a collection of Appalachian poetry I wrote, and explained *why* I wrote and how I chose my subjects. Then I showed them a videotaped interview of Verna Mae Slone done for one of my college writing classes. At the end of the interview, I read them a poem of mine about family. "Knowing My Place" was inspired by a George Ella Lyon poem, "Where I'm From." I wrote about my childhood and about those who influenced me when I was growing up. I described my childhood toys and play activities much as James Still does in his autobiographical poem "Those I Want in Heaven With Me Should There Be Such a Place." In one line I described the only new bicycle I ever owned and the coal trucks I had to avoid while riding it on the narrow Sitka road beside my home:

It took dying for me to know
Where I'm from.
It took dying for me to clearly see.
Upon dying, I knew my place.

In the blinding white light
I saw I'm from
Back roads ridden miles on magenta bicycle,
Dodging red fifties coal trucks.

From old four-room houses
Made into warm hogars.
Only in later years
Would I understand their similarity to another culture's homes.

From two-family, two-front-doored,
Square-cut log home

In white trimmed black and white photos,
Hidden in shoebox coffins, ashamed to be shown.

From "He has his mother's love for learning."
She who like so many in her day
Chose to stay in the eighth grade two years,
Knowing a higher education was out of reach.

From Monnie and Jasper,
Millard and Zory,
Miners and farmers and all-day working wives and mothers,
Orchards and tobacco bases and deep mine tunnels.

From Van Lear and Virginia,
Hood's creek and Scotland's highlands,
Hollows and holly filled
Stands of Black Virginia pine.

From home healings
And growing and living by the signs,
Quiet turns
And well-known tempers.

From slate falls
And Paintsville Hospital stays,
Wheelchairs
And Pikeville Miners' Hospital black lung treatments.

It took dying to see where I'm from.
It took dying for me to
Finally
Know my place.

I told the children to write about those people and events that had made a special impact on their lives. They put their heads down, and a few began to write freely, quickly filling up the page. I walked over beside one little boy who was not writing. He was too shy to tell me his name, so his older sister answered for him, trying to take care of him, as she was accustomed to doing. I suggested that he begin writing about his grandparents.

When time was up, I let each read in turn and discovered some excellent stories filled with rich detail much the same as Mrs. Slone's. These children loved writing. No one had, as of yet, been critical of their writing. They had listened to Verna Mae Slone tell them to write from their hearts and not to worry about pleasing others. Most enjoyed the chance to write about their families, but I was left to wonder about those who came up with nothing.

I later was humbled to discover that the good participation I received in my workshop was at least in part due to the fact that my former student was evaluating their participation and behavior on a point system, and only those with high point totals would be allowed to go swimming at the city park that afternoon. Still, many of these eight to eleven-year-olds enjoyed sharing their stories through their poems. They modeled close detail, and many proudly shared what they had written—unafraid of criticism just as Mrs. Slone and I had encouraged them to be.

Just as I ask of my students, I read my writing to my college students today with no fear of rejection or discouragement. That was not the case in the past. Many teachers would never share their writing with their students for fear that some would make disparaging remarks. Jesse Stuart read his drafts to his students often, and although he disliked it when his students gave his writing the thumbs down, he had to later admit that they were correct much more often than they were wrong and that the stories they approved of were publishable more often than not.

Moving beyond the fear of reading my own work to my students has helped not only my writing but my teaching as well. If I am to form a *community* of writers, how can I participate in that community fully without reading my writing to my students just as I ask them to read their writing to their peers and to me? On the first day of classes each term, I explain that all writing is a process, and that although improvement is essential, perfection is impossible to achieve. In order to illustrate this, I pull from my pocket a small amethyst stone and hand it to a student to pass around the classroom. I ask the students to roll the stone around in their hands and tell me what they discover. The stone has a flaw. Its surface is not perfectly smooth. I explain that I carry this stone with me always as a reminder that we are all just doing the best we can and that nothing will ever be perfect. It helps put me at ease as I teach and as I share my writing with my students. I must create an atmosphere in the classroom in which students and I are not afraid of failure, for without making mistakes we would not be human and we would have no potential to improve.

I tell my students about "Stick Stories," a poem I first published in 1997. In the poem I tell the true story of the time I stopped alongside old Route 23 between Paintsville and Prestonsburg to barter with a Martin County peddler for a walking stick. The stick was unusual, for it was made from a dogwood limb. The limb had been stripped of its bark to reveal a corkscrew effect formed from its entanglement with a grape vine. In the poem I explain that I did not just buy the walking stick; I also bought the maker's *story*. He would not sell it to me unless I listened to the story of finding the branch and stripping and shaping it into the walking stick. As I looked closely at the dogwood walking stick, I thought of the story of the crucifixion and the Christian symbolism of the dogwood tree—its ivory bloom in the shape of the cross, petals stained blood red. I also thought of the irony of turning the dogwood limb into a walking stick—that is supposed to *support* the walker, for everyone knows the dogwood is too spindly and weak to support the body's weight.

I close the poem with a line that continues to please me these many years after writing the poem: "He liked leaning on *stories*." I explain to my students that the craftsman gave me his story, reminded me of the Biblical story, and provided me with a story poem—all for the price of my having taken the time to listen and the three dollars I paid him. Students enjoy hearing about the "history" of a piece of writing. They learn to become aware of their surroundings and to take the time to listen to stories themselves. Students today too often do not take the time to notice details.

I wrote the poem "Stick Stories" and kept re-writing it until it became the published poem they see today. Furthermore, I could not have written it well without the help of feedback and criticism from those I read it to as it was a work in progress. For example, one line reads: "His right foot was on the brake before his brain knew why." In the early drafts of the poem, my *left* foot hit the brake, not my right. I read the poem to a group of students, and one bright young lady wanted to know why I stepped on the brake pedal with my left foot instead of my right. She had never heard of anyone using *both* feet to drive unless there was a clutch involved. She was correct of course, and without her help, I would have published a poem lying to the world that I push the brake pedal with my left foot instead of my *right*. If I had been afraid of making a mistake, and if that fear had prevented me from reading the poem to my students, I would have surely made the mistake for the world to see.

There have been other times when sharing my writing with my students has saved me. I once wrote a poem about Mrs. Ilene Hampton, my fourth-grade teacher. I thought it was a beautiful tribute to her, but in the poem I imagined her in death extending her hand to put a piece of chalk in my hand. I read the poem to my students, and next class meeting time, a student came to my desk to tell me that Mrs. Hampton was a neighbor of hers on Little Mud Lick and that she was still very much alive. "Would I please revise the poem and not refer to her as having *died*?" was the request Mrs. Hampton sent to me through her neighbor. *Learning* from our mistakes does not stop with the earning of a degree. We are all a part of a community where we are meant to help one another.

CHAPTER NINE

The fact that we are a part of a *community* never becomes so apparent as when we stop to offer thanks. When we stop to think of the times we have said thank-you to those who were not related to us for help received, we are made aware that we were part of a community. After students read their papers aloud in my writing classes, their classmates are required to answer a questionnaire called a "Peer Response." One of the questions is "What did the writer do in this paper that I might try in my own writing in order to improve?" The last requirement is that the reviewers write a personal statement to the writer about the paper. For example, reviewers might write that they could relate their own life experiences to the stories heard.

A descriptive paper recently read in one of my classes took the reader into an Old Regular Baptist funeral. Songs mentioned evoked memories of funeral services others in class had attended. Dani, my female student, described the way the funeral director stood to wave his hand in the direction of the casket and the pulpit so that family members might go forward first for their last viewing of her papaw. She described the long walk she took up the aisle to see for the last time her papaw's glasses that never did fit him properly and to hold her papaw's hand. Memories came flooding back for my students and for me.

The focus of the peer response is on content, tone, and voice.

Ken Slone, first year teacher, 1975.

Students are not proficient at helping one another with writing mechanics. That's where I step in. Near the end of class, I sit down beside the students whose papers were heard and reviewed that day and show them where grammatical and punctuation improvements are needed. Most of the time when I finish helping students in this way, they turn to say: "Thank you, Mr. Slone." I know when they do so, I have begun to form a community of writers.

Expressions of gratitude often come unexpectedly. Almost three years after I left northern Kentucky and returned to the mountains to teach, I received a special invitation. My former students in Gallatin County invited me to return to be their commencement speaker. I had not realized that I would miss teaching high school students when I accepted the offer to teach for the University of Kentucky Community College system. I had missed my students though and had wondered how they were doing and where they had decided to attend college. I was senior class sponsor for three consecutive years prior to leaving. I missed giving the annual informal speech to graduates who were preparing to practice for the ceremony. I always told them that commencement was for their parents and grandparents as much as for them. Their thoughts as they rehearsed and on the actual evening of commencement should be focused on their people—the sacrifices they had made and the support they had given. I suppose I gave much the same speech on the stage at Gallatin County High when I returned to be their guest speaker, but it's not the speech itself that I remember. After students received their diplomas, it was tradition in Gallatin County that the graduates would all stand and throw their caps into the air. Usually graduates would make a quick exit from the gymnasium. This year caps flew into the air as usual, but the graduates did not leave. Instead they lined up to shake my hand and offer thanks. I stood there for an hour and a half speaking to my former students who were not just happy to see me but were there to say thank you—not for returning to be their speaker but for having been their teacher. I will never forget those thank-yous.

I also remember those thank-yous I have given over the years to those outside my family who became *family* to me through their kindnesses. One example of a time I realized that I was a part of a community of folks who supported me—one of those times I said thank-you—was during the spring of 1971, my final semester at Johnson Central High School. I was in line to be valedictorian of a class of approximately 260 students. My father had no savings. He did not even have a checking account. I remember my father would sit at the kitchen table every payday Saturday afternoon trying to find a way to stretch his weekly paycheck in order to pay for our groceries, the electric bill, and the bills in town at stores like S and S Shoe Store and Pinky's where he bought his work clothes and my brother's and my jeans. All his bills he paid by cash each week. If he ever received a written account of a bill in the mail, he became very angry. He called these written statements, which he considered to be demands for payment "duns," and he cursed those who had "dunned" him. He felt as if he should be trusted to remember the debts he owed. I remember if I made noise while he was counting out the money for bills, he would reprimand me sternly. I learned to be quiet and to leave him alone until long after his money counting was over and his mind was once again on something else.

My teachers knew that I would be the first in my family to go to college, and they knew my parents could not afford to send me. I did farm work for one dollar an hour, and I found a job working at Frail's, a men's clothing store in Paintsville where I could make a dollar and a quarter an hour, but that would just be enough to help me with books and food—not enough for tuition and housing.

I decided to visit Eastern Kentucky University. I had heard about scholarships there, awarded to high school seniors who were at the top of their class. I soon discovered that EKU was not offering this scholarship to Johnson Central students because administrators did not consider my high school to be a part of their service area. They thought, and rightly so, that most students who were graduating from Johnson Central would attend Morehead State University. I had visited EKU's campus as a band member when we had been invited to play during a halftime show at a football game. I knew of the reputation EKU had for training teachers and thought by going to college in central Kentucky I could meet students from all over the state and all over the world. (I was correct. I would later have a roommate, Peter Yen Wai Ming, from Hong Kong.) Disappointed upon finding out that I would not receive a scholarship, I visited the only person on the campus whom I knew: EKU Bursar, Bill Stapleton. Mr. Stapleton was a former superintendent of schools in my home county. He knew my family and my circumstances. I remember he asked me directly, "Are you serious about wanting to attend Eastern Kentucky University?" When I said yes, he said, "Come with me." We walked down the hall and up the stairs in the Coates Administration Building to the financial aid office where he made sure I was offered a grant and a matching loan that would be enough to pay for my tuition and dorm room for the first year. My grant and aid amount was renewable each year contingent upon my grades. Then Mr. Stapleton took me in his car for a tour of the campus. I learned that the college was laid out in a square surrounding "the ravine," a natural amphitheatre in the center of campus. He proudly pointed out sites where new buildings like the university chapel and the Wallace Building were to be constructed. The thank-you I gave Mr. Stapleton felt insufficient to repay him for his kindness. I would call on him many times throughout my college years at EKU. He was the first person I spoke with when I was drafted into the service. These were the Viet Nam years. Deferments for college were ending, and the Selective Service was calling up young men based on a lottery system. My birthday fell on lottery pick number sixty-one.

Bill Stapleton proved to me that my community was larger than I knew. It extended to Richmond, Kentucky. I met my wife Debbie there where we planned our future. Mr. Stapleton and so many others—faculty like Dr. Michael Bright and Dr. Richard Clarkson and friends—made EKU a family and Richmond, Kentucky a place that will always feel like home.

CHAPTER TEN

Big Sandy Community and Technical College and my home are near Route 23, which stretches north and south through the far eastern part of Kentucky. Each county that the four-lane passes through lays claim to its share of country or bluegrass musicians. In the effort to pay the artists tribute as well as to capitalize on the artists' national and in some cases international fame, Kentucky's tourism bureau has posted highway signs on county borderlines, designating each county as the home of its famous entertainer(s). Stars such as Loretta Lynn, Crystal Gayle, Hylo Brown, Wynonna Judd, Naomi Judd, Billy Ray Cyrus, Ricky Skaggs, Dwight Yaokam, Patty Loveless, and Gary Stewart all called the counties along Route 23 in east Kentucky home.

Music has had its impact on my students in this region. Performers from the mountains pay tribute to the influence of hearing traditional hymns, sung in mountain churches, upon their own singing styles. Today the Paramount Arts Center in Ashland and the Mountain Arts Center in Prestonsburg host performances including but not limited to artists with roots in the mountains. Students in the mountains have the opportunity to see homecoming concerts performed by singers and songwriters from the counties through which Route 23 passes as well as artists from other nearby east Kentucky counties such as Carter County's Tom T. Hall, Morgan County's

Don Rigsby, and Magoffin County's Charlie Sizemore.

Charlie Sizemore was one of my students. Charlie had traveled the world performing with Bluegrass legend Ralph Stanley. He played lead guitar and sang harmony with Ralph as had his predecessor Keith Whitley, before Keith began his solo career. Both Keith and Charlie sang the part that Ralph's brother Carter had sung with the original Stanley Brothers band. Carter could put more *feeling* into his songs than any other country or bluegrass artist of his time. Grown men would be moved to tears upon hearing his songs. Carter's influence can be heard in both artists who replaced him. Ralph and Carter performed what Ralph calls the "old-time mountain sound." Their songs were a part of the recent movie *O Brother, Where Art Thou?* Ralph and other artists featured in the soundtrack performed traditional songs that formed the foundation of today's country music.

Anyone who has lived and taught in the mountains cannot help but hear the influence of the Old Regular/ United Baptist hymn singing in Ralph Stanley's style. He *lifts* the last part of each line just as the United Baptists do when they sing the words lined out for them without musical accompaniment.

Mornings on my papaw Slone's farm began with an early awakening. I slept alongside an open window—weather permitting. When roosters' crows did not wake me, I would wake to the sweet sound of my mamaw's singing. She sang as she stirred in the kitchen preparing a country breakfast. Unlike my parents, she did not listen to Bill Barker's morning radio program; she sang her *own* songs to accompany her biscuit making. She sang hymns she had learned from the old blue *Thomas Hymnal* or *Sweet Songster*—songs she had sung in the Hood's Creek United Baptist Church where she was a member.

In United Baptist churches these hymns would be "lined out."

A song leader like my papaw would speak the words first. Then the congregation would join in singing the words he had spoken with power and feeling. No instrumentation ever accompanied the singing. So much feeling and *power* could be put into this style of singing that musical accompaniment was not needed. Besides, tradition forbade the playing of musical instruments in the church. Words cannot explain the *grace* with which my mamaw sang those hymns. Each line she sang seemed to lift the words toward Heaven. Her soprano voice would lilt as she approached the end of each line of verse, her words purling upward toward the sky. I wondered how anyone could be so happy so early in the morning. She was filled with the spirit of thankfulness for the new day God had given her. My papaw enjoyed the recognition he received from folks who came to visit just to hear him sing. My mamaw didn't think anyone was listening to *her*, but I was.

If all of the singers and songwriters who grew up near US 23, the Country Music Highway, were asked whether they heard Old Regular or United Baptist singing when they were children, I'm sure the answer would be yes. Even if they did not attend church regularly, United or Old Regular Baptist funeral services were likely forever etched into their memories. Many have memories, like mine, of hearing a grandparent singing those old hymns at home. Those born and raised in the mountains, who know those hymns as I do, can recognize their influence on modern Bluegrass and country artists. Just listen to the *feeling* that Ricky Skaggs puts into his song "Little Bessie," for example. Except for the instruments' accompaniment, he could be singing inside a Lawrence County United Baptist churchhouse. Patty Loveless from Pike County sings, "You'll Never Leave Harlan Alive," with that same feeling. It was impossible to live in the Big Sandy River valley and *not* hear United

Baptist lined-out hymns if you were born here in the fifties, sixties, or seventies. If you never attended a Sunday morning service or funeral, you could hear them Sundays on mountain radio taped broadcasts. Those hymns have a drawing power that attracts listeners and a spiritual affirmation that can connect the singers with one another and with those who listen. All become *close*.

East Kentucky students are surprised to learn that in 1997 Smithsonian Folkways in Washington DC produced a CD recording of Old Regular Baptist Hymns titled "Songs of the Old Regular Baptists—Lined-out Hymnody From Southeastern Kentucky." I explain to my students that this type of singing originated in sixteenth-century Scotland and Ireland, where many of their ancestors lived and worshipped, and from there was introduced into the mountains of southwestern Virginia where many Scots Irish migrated and eventually on into what is today eastern Kentucky. Many students have heard the erroneous story that lined-out singing began because east Kentucky churches were so poor that they could not afford to purchase enough hymnals for everyone in the congregation. East Kentuckians have allowed outsiders who do not understand the culture and traditions of mountain people to explain away their inheritance. The true story is one of a beautiful tradition that has survived in a region where tradition is sacred, and purity and simplicity have been historically valued.

Members of the Indian Bottom Association of Old Regular Baptists at Defeated Creek Church, Linefork, in Pike County sing on the recording, hymns such as "Jesus, Thou Art the Sinner's Friend" in the same powerful, emotional, lined-out style that my grandparents used to sing that hymn. The last track on the CD is most special. It provides an excellent resource for anyone who wants to teach the importance of passion in creativity. The singers each take turns expressing what this type of singing means to them and telling stories from their childhood of hearing their people sing these songs. They express the desire that this tradition may be carried on through the generations. One singer says he likes to read the lyrics as *poetry* because they sound pretty. Their stories themselves are often poetic although the church members probably have never written poems. One says that the sound of the old hymns seems to be "carried by the trees off the hill-top cemetery memorial service and down into the valley below." One speaker explains that he drives a shuttle car in the mines. When the continuous miner breaks down, and all the men gather round to tell lies and fish stories, he begins singing Old Regular Baptist hymns.

A silence falls over the classroom as singers take turns telling their stories. I can feel the *respect* my students are paying not only to these singers but to their parents and grandparents as well, in honor of whom these stories are told. If I see a student who is uncomfortable listening to these emotional testimonies and songs, I can be certain that student is also uncomfortable with his or her cultural heritage, and that saddens me because it will be a burden that young man or woman will bear for a lifetime. As one Pike County Old Regular Baptist proudly said it best: "These are our people. This is our culture."

As a boy I went to see Ralph Stanley's band at a little one-room schoolhouse. We sat in wooden student desks around a pot-bellied coal stove, and the singing that reverberated throughout the little oil-floored classroom made its way inside us all. Those were days when country and bluegrass were losing popularity in favor of rock and roll. Performers were forced to play wherever there was an audience, no matter the size.

Charlie Sizemore began playing the fiddle when he was six. No one he knew played the fiddle so he taught himself. Curly Ray Cline, with whom he later worked in Ralph's band, taught him how to play "Wednesday Night Waltz," which is still one of Charlie's favorite tunes. Charlie's father played guitar and banjo and taught him how to play guitar when Charlie was twelve. He learned to play drop-thumb style banjo from his grandfather Hager. The first band that Charlie performed with was "Lum Patton and the Half Mountain Boys."

Charlie was with Ralph Stanley's band in the late seventies and early eighties when even college students were warming to country and bluegrass music. Lester Flatt and Earl Scruggs and Ralph and Charlie performed on college campuses as well as at large bluegrass festivals all over the nation, and even overseas—especially in Germany and Japan where their traditional style of music was mimicked and enjoyed.

Charlie wrote in an early journal entry for my writing class that he "didn't want to spend the rest of his life without an education, traveling around the country in the back of a bus," so he quit the band, enrolled in college, and began pursuit of his degree.

While attending college classes, he still continued his music career, but he did so as a solo performer so that he could set his own schedule and begin recording and performing while obtaining his degree. The Charlie Sizemore Band would travel only short distances and often open for artists such as Vern Gosden who were on national tours themselves.

Ironically Charlie, who was perfectly at ease on stage in front of thousands of fans, was nervous walking into class that first day wearing his boot-cut jeans, cowboy boots. and western-cut shirt. His first contact with our college was through his friend, Tom

Whitaker, who had known Charlie and his family since Charlie was a little boy playing on Puncheon Creek in Magoffin County. I understand how Charlie felt. Just as Mr. Bill Stapleton helped me, Tom must have been a tremendous help to Charlie as he made the transition into college. I'm likewise sure that I have Tom to thank for recommending that Charlie take my class.

Charlie began to feel at ease in my class when he realized that he was not the only non-traditional student. Soon he was competing to be the best writer in the group. He did not have to be taught that the best writing comes from life experiences. He enjoyed the limelight when I read one of his papers as an example of the kind of writing I was looking for, and probably then and there planted the seeds for a change in my teaching style that would permit students to take pride in writing papers about life experiences.

A conversation about the music business he had on board Tom T. Hall's bus with Tom's brother was the subject of a journal entry. In 2002, Charlie and Tom T. Hall performed together on a CD, a collection of songs Tom wrote called *The Story Is—The Songs of Tom T. Hall*. On the cover Charlie is seated at a bar holding a drink while Tom T. Hall, the bartender, shines glasses behind the bar.

In addition to being a songwriter and performer, Tom T. Hall is a writer of short stories. I remember a lesson Charlie especially enjoyed. I used a Tom T. Hall short story titled "The Gate" from a collection of stories called *The Acts of Life*. A young man who had always aspired to be a writer pays a visit to the only writer in his community. As he approaches the writer's house, he comes upon the place where there was once a fence. All that remains is the gate. The aspiring writer stands before the gate. He sees that the shortest, most direct path to the door is not through the standing gate but through the place where the fence once stood. Instead of taking the easiest path, he opens the gate, steps through, and closes the gate behind him.

The old writer who greets him looks nothing at all like the young man had expected. His clothes are as disheveled as the inside of his home. There are no bookshelves lining the walls, and no typewriter rests in front of a wide window, just a Formica dining room table with four mismatched chairs. The old writer sees the look of obvious disappointment on the young man's face. He says that when we envision a writer, we see the writer seated in his comfortable leather chair in front of a cherry desk. A pipe rests in its cradle beside a typewriter. A glass of sherry sits on a small table to the side of his chair. On the other side a Labrador retriever naps on an antique rug. The chair faces an over-sized window where he can see cardinals and blue jays darting in and out of a mature white pine. A tall rhododendron in late spring bloom is there beneath the pine.

The old writer destroys the aspiring writer's dream and explains that in fact his best writing is done in the bathroom. He opens the bathroom door and says that this is where he writes. The young writer thanks the old man for his time and leaves the way he came, opening the gate and closing it behind him.

Once he is gone, Tom T. Hall writes that the old man opens the door to an office with a leather chair, a cherry desk, a dog, a typewriter, and an oversized window. He sits down in the comfortable chair, picks up his pipe, tamps in some fresh tobacco and thinks about the young man. Just then his maid enters the room and complains to him about how harsh she heard him be with the boy. "Oh, he is going to be alright. He will become a writer some day without any encouragement from me. He came in through the gate."

When I used this story as a model for teaching metaphor, I kept the author a secret in the beginning. I thought my students would stereotype Tom T. Hall as a country singer and have a difficult time thinking of him as writer of short stories. I underestimated them. Tom T. Hall is known as *The Story Teller*. I wonder if Charlie thought of that short story as he decided to record the 2002 released CD, *The Story Is—The Songs of Tom T. Hall*.

Charlie's life experience-based papers continued throughout the two semesters he was in my writing classes. He wrote about appearing for the first time on the stage of the Ryman Auditorium for the Grand Old Opry. He wrote a lesson paper about buying his first Cadillac. The moral to his classmates and me was: Cadillacs rust and break down just like any other cars. The shine of a new Cadillac soon fades, and the money, once paid never returns, so don't waste your money. He wrote about the songwriting business, describing it as it really is— a *business* where songwriters are placed with other songwriters in a closet-like room under pressure to produce according to a time clock. His writing did wonders to shatter the idealistic illusions of his classmates just as the old writer did in Tom T. Hall's short story, "The Gate."

Charlie completed his two-year associate's degree at Prestonsburg Community College, now Big Sandy Community and Technical College, and then transferred to the University of Kentucky where his major was political science/pre-law. He obtained his law degree from the Nashville School of Law and today has his own appellate and trial law practice. His wife Robin also began her education at Big Sandy Community and Technical College, has earned her master's degree, and is teaching second grade in Goodlettsville near Nashville.

Charlie is off the road that he traveled for some twenty-one years, but still recording, writing, and performing from time to time. In October 2003, he returned to perform at the Mountain Arts Center in a benefit concert supporting scholarships for Big Sandy Community College students. Beth Sizemore, Charlie's niece, was a recent student of mine. She once brought to class his favorite bluegrass song "Bristlecone Pine." The bristlecone pine is said to be the oldest living tree. The deeply spiritual song expresses the attachment to place that one feels in coming from the mountains. The song is my personal favorite. Beth let Charlie know that I was in the audience. He sang the song for me, and after the show I stayed to thank him. Another song he performed, "Back Home," he said was written in Lexington soon after he left Big Sandy Community and Technical College. In it is a longing for the home place, a longing that Charlie gives in to from time to time when he returns home to visit family and friends.

His people have not forgotten him. Not many years ago, they arranged a benefit concert in his honor at the local football field. He was still in school without medical insurance and needed an operation, so Melvin Goins, a local promoter and long-time Bluegrass entertainer, organized a benefit concert for Charlie. Bill Monroe, Tom T. Hall, Allison Kraus, and Ralph Stanley among others all came to perform with no stipend so that their musician-and-songwriter friend could afford the operation he needed.

"Bristlecone Pine" is the song Charlie told his niece he wanted to be sung at his funeral. The song is a wonderful symbol of Charlie's life. He will always be rooted to the mountains and to the storytelling tradition. As if to emphasize *storytelling*, the storyteller himself, Tom T. Hall, walked on stage at the Mountain Arts Center to sing his song "I Love..." and to introduce Charlie to the fans he had come home to entertain. Tom T. Hall is retired from the music business and enjoying life on his farm, but he stepped out of retirement to introduce his long-time friend.

Charlie played guitar and sang harmony with Ralph Stanley nine years, replacing the late Keith Whitley. Keith Whitley's songs are today as popular around the world as in his native east Kentucky. Keith Whitley's Elliott County home is only a few miles from Route 23. Songwriting and performing are part of the culture of the mountain people.

Keith's singing and songwriting, like Charlie's, were done with *feeling*. He did not just *say* the words. I learned about putting feeling into the words of a song and into the playing of an instrument by sitting on the front porch of my grandparents' home and listening to my cousin James Isom Slone sing or play the fiddle. He lived in a suburb of Dayton, Ohio, where he, like my father, had migrated to find a factory job just after World War II, but he would pack his fiddle and return to Johnson County as often as he could. I remember he always pulled a white handkerchief from his pocket to place against the fiddle to cushion his chin as it rested on the instrument. As I watched him play, I was learning what it was like to put feeling into playing an instrument.

James Isom would close his eyes and *become* the fiddle. He would *feel* the melody line come through him and out through the instrument. The handkerchief came in handy as beads of sweat were soon to appear on his forehead, and in between tunes he would stop to relax a moment and wipe them away. Later in his life, his wife would not let him bring his fiddle on visits. He had developed heart problems, and she was afraid that he would put so much emotion into his playing that he would raise his blood pressure and trigger a heart attack.

I still owned my first guitar in those days. On one of my cousin's visits, I remember when I played a tune for him, he complimented me and encouraged me to continue playing. He said I had a good sense of rhythm as I strummed the guitar. I would remember his compliment as I sat alone on my bed practicing.

My father could play one song on the guitar all the way through. I would listen to him play the first line of a song, expecting it to continue, but was always disappointed to hear him stop after the first line. The only song he knew all the way through was "Wildwood Flower." It was the first song I learned to play of course, and it was the song I played for my talented Ohio cousin. The compliment he gave me has influenced my teaching. I take the time to write a note of praise in the margin when I see reason to encourage. Students accept criticisms better if they are accompanied by a compliment.

One of my students knew Faye Whitley, Keith's mother, who still lives in Keith's hometown of Sandy Hook, Kentucky. My student was planning to conduct an interview with her and needed some help thinking of questions that would be appropriate for the interview. I asked the class to help by thinking of two questions that they would like her to answer about Keith's background and career. I was surprised to find several students who could not stop with two. One turned in two pages of questions, explaining that she owned every CD that Keith had recorded.

Mrs. Whitley said in her interview that her son's stage career began when at age four he performed in a talent contest at a Lawrence County grade school. She showed a picture of him dressed in a cowboy outfit and holding a ukulele, flat side up, as one would hold a dobro (acoustic steel guitar). She remembered the song he sang that night, "Big Iron" and how much the audience enjoyed his singing, so much that they yelled for him to sing the song again when it ended the first time. She said Keith sang from the heart. He would listen to George Jones and to Ralph and Carter Stanley. In their voices, he heard the importance of "feeling" the words of the song as he performed. When "Big Iron" ended the second time, the audience stood to applaud his performance. Needless to say, he won the talent competition.

As did many young people growing up in the mountains, Keith learned to play by ear and from imitating family members. His grandfather played guitar as did Faye, his mother. His uncle played the banjo. Playing music was popular in the mountains in a time when there was little other entertainment than listening to a floor model radio. Battery radios preceded rural electric cooperatives and the arrival of electricity into the homes of rural east Kentucky residents. Not every family had one, but the homes of those who did have radios were very popular—especially on Saturday nights when the Grand Ole Opry would be aired live from the Ryman Auditorium on 650-WSM in Nashville. Listening to the Grand Ole Opry, boys and girls could dream of themselves singing on that stage some day. All singers and songwriters from east Kentucky will point to the listening of the Saturday night Opry as the inspiration for their desire to learn to play and sing. Keith was no exception.

His mother told the story of her son's first big break in the music business. In the sixties country music had superseded Bluegrass in popularity, and Bluegrass performers like Ralph Stanley and Bill Monroe were forced to perform wherever they could. I remember going to the Sky View Drive-In movie theatre in Paintsville to watch Bluegrass musicians perform. I would sit on my mother's lap to see through the windshield. The musicians would stand on the roof of the projection/concession building, and the sound would come through the movie sound speakers that hung on our side glass car windows. There were no soundboards and loudspeaker systems in those days.

Musicians would also perform in elementary schools. It was at a talent show in one of these schools that Keith Whitley and Ricky Skaggs were performing while everyone waited on Ralph and his band to arrive. They had had a flat tire and were delayed. When they approached the schoolhouse, Ralph commented that someone was playing one of their records because he thought he heard himself and his brother Carter singing. Upon entering the building, he saw that it was not a recording but that Keith and Ricky were playing and singing *their* songs. Ralph asked Faye if Keith could begin traveling and performing with his band on weekends, and so began his career at age twelve.

Creativity is a difficult process to define, but Faye Whitley described Keith's songwriting as best she could. He would receive an inspiration and go into his bedroom to write the song. He loved to sit on his bed and play his guitar. One day he came out of his room and told her he had a song he wanted her to hear. It was titled "Great High Mountain," and from it she recalled the words: "You Don't Have to Move That Mountain. Help Me Lord to Climb It." Even though she said she had no favorite song that he had written, she was very proud of this song in particular because so many different artists recorded it. Keith also played in their old garage where on Wednesday nights he and Ricky Skaggs taped a gospel radio show broadcast each weekend on the Grayson, Kentucky, radio station. People would come from miles away to crowd into that garage and listen to their songs.

One of the questions asked of Faye was about Keith's love for Elliott County and the people who lived there. She said when he returned to the Frosty Freeze restaurant, he would sign autographs for all who wanted them no matter how much time it took. He never forgot his roots. He even recorded a video in his hometown. His popularity was not limited to Sandy Hook, Kentucky. He traveled and performed around the world, and Faye told us he was especially popular in Japan. "They would tie my shoes for me if I would let them," he had told her.

As many as sixty fans in one day still come by her home to talk with her. She proudly shows them her son's photos and keepsakes. Keith gave her his guitar shortly before he died, and that guitar today rests just where it should, on his bed, as if he might return to sit there and write another song.

Mountain students are encouraged by the fact that artists such as Charlie Sizemore, Tom T. Hall and Keith Whitley, with backgrounds similar to their own, have realized their dreams. They learn from their examples to be proud of their culture.

CHAPTER ELEVEN

Good teaching is done in a community of good teachers. I have had the good fortune to teach alongside so many excellent, caring teachers during the past thirty years that I cannot begin to name them all. I cannot attempt a listing, for in doing so I would certainly leave out someone who deserves to be included. Please allow the following story to illustrate an example of the collegial relationships I have had during my teaching career.

In the Magoffin Building on the campus of Big Sandy Community and Technical College there is an art gallery. Our founding president, Dr. Henry A. Campbell, Jr., in the plans for the new building insisted there should be an open-glass design of an art gallery. He was perhaps led to this decision by hiring in the early seventies a young artist from Puncheon Creek in Magoffin County named Tom J. Whitaker.

Tom describes his first meeting with Doc (as everyone on campus called him). It was a unique experience. Doc told Tom that he had hired four art teachers in a span of nine years, and that they all had some extreme character flaw. The second-to-the-last never changed his clothing and lived in a van, and the last one was a psychotic who dressed only in black. "And just what is wrong with you?" Doc asked Tom. Knowing Tom the way I do, I'm sure he had a comeback and that his reply was a straightforward one, for that is how Tom is. I also suspect that Tom's honesty is the quality that Dr. Campbell admired most. In those days you were hired at Prestonsburg Community College, the first in the University of Kentucky Community College system, solely on the basis of a personal interview done by Doc himself in his own unique style.

A walk down the first-floor hallway of the Pike Building now likely brings about an encounter with Appalachia's greatest artist, Tom J. Whitaker. He can usually be found in the art studio surrounded by the clutter that says "Here is the studio of a working artist." If you don't step inside the studio, you will be greeted as you pass with a "Hello, brother!" and made to feel that if you do not take the time to step in, you are living your life in far too much of a hurry. Tom is never in a hurry. He always has the time to find the important subjects to talk about with you— those that lie just beneath the surface of the "I'm fine" reply you give to others who may pass you by quickly on campus, asking how you are but not really wanting to know.

Tom's advice is freely given upon request. I remember when I published my first book of poems, he laughed at the number of copies I planned to have printed and encouraged me to print more. How he knew that the Pikeville printer would go out of business and that today two copies of the book would be all that remain of that first printing, I will never know. His encouragement seemed based on unrealistic expectations, but through years of printing copies of his art he had a feel for what the public wanted and would pay for. For example, I remember once he told me he would never again print a painting of a church. " A particular churchhouse is a spiritual symbol only for the members who attend there. No one else will want to buy a print of it," he said.

Tom paints what his experience has led him to discover. A writer

Portrait of Tom J. Whitaker
Title—The Artist

may carry a pen and notepad in order to record ideas for his writing. Tom carries a camera and a vivid memory. He has an eye for the penetrating beauty in an old man's eyes, the lifetime of hard work story-told in his bowed back, or the sun-darkened, wrinkled skin on his hands. Tom's art is like a work of literature that one can return to again and again to find new symbols and new meanings the artist/writer had hoped you would discover.

I first met Tom just after I had been hired to teach by Dr. Campbell. I had just moved my family into a new home in my native county and was taking a walk through Paintsville, the county seat I had grown up in, when I came upon Tom and some other artists displaying their work in front of the courthouse. My interest was first directed toward the man and not toward his art. He was dressed in a bright red shirt and blue jeans, and even on this warm June day wore a black, wide-brimmed bohemian style hat. He was making easy conversation with prospective customers, his hands waving as he spoke. From him my focus shifted to a watercolor painting of a weathered brown house with a rusted tin roof framed by a falling split rail fence and Virginia black pines. A white gravel approach led up the fencerow toward the front door. A wooden well box with rope and pulley and bucket were beside the back door. There were holes where windowpanes once had been, and the screen door was slightly ajar. I didn't know why I was attracted to the painting at the time, but I was, so I purchased it from him without explaining that I would be teaching with him soon.

I later hung the painting on my office wall, and one day Tom noticed it there. He remembered it and our first conversation, but he shuddered at its appearance now, for I had framed it myself using a recycled Dollar Store frame. Its mat was disproportionately cut surrounding the painting which itself was set crooked in the cheap frame. Tom talked the division secretary into loaning him a master key, probably saying he had forgotten his office key, used it to get inside my office, took the ill-framed painting from my wall back to his studio in order to frame it with winter-sky-blue mat. Tom titled the painting *Memories from the Hills*. In 2001 it caught the eye of Brett Nance and Jim Gifford at the Jesse Stuart Foundation and was used on a reprinting of a collection of Jesse Stuart's short stories, titled *Come Back to the Farm*. I smiled as I watched the opening of the *KET Bookclub* program on which Stuart's book was to be discussed. Bill Goodman and his panel first complimented the book's cover, the painting that had first caught *my* eye that summer day on the Johnson County courthouse lawn. I have since discovered that for me the painting represents the old tenant farmer's shack where I lived until I was six.

The attraction to Tom Whitaker's art begins with an interest in the man himself and then drifts off to the side to his paintings. What touches your spirit about the man and his art is at first *felt* and only later understood. The *eyes* of Tom's characters draw you in. They might be the eyes of a loved one. Perhaps they are a woman's eyes— my grandmother Slone's. Or they could be the eyes of my papaw Huff, my mother's father.

Tom often presents to my class or grants an interview for a

student's cultural presentation. In one such class presentation done in the spring of 2000, Tom talked of the importance of *feeling*. His words were, "I tell you I don't believe anything anybody says. I believe what I *feel* about what they say. When I go to church, I don't believe the words of the preacher, I believe what I *feel* about those words."

We in Appalachia tend to be thought of in terms of our likenesses, but to Tom our *differences* make us special. He walks into a classroom and feels the strength of his students' differences. Again, it is the *feeling* that is important whether students are learning from Tom or from one another, or whether Tom is learning from his students. Learning is like that. It takes place in all directions.

Tom realized that there are different worlds in the mountains and that those worlds are far apart. *His* first world was the one of his earliest memories—being raised on Puncheon Creek in Magoffin County. That may have been the most beautiful world of all. Residents were all together as extended family. His grandpa kept the family together, and there would be family get-togethers on holidays and even on Sundays when there *were* no holidays. Tom was describing the idea of being among a *community* of people who cared about you and made you feel special. Some have chosen to limit their world to their own Puncheon Creeks, but Tom, like so many other Appalachians, left that world for larger and more complicated ones. He first discovered Royalton and learned to gamble there. Then his world expanded into the Magoffin County seat Salyersville, and along with new *places* his world expanded to new people with new sets of values.

Tom grew up among the strongest influences in his life— his two grandmothers, and he echoed James Still's words by saying, "Women have always been the true leaders of Appalachia. They just do not get the credit." His grandmother Whitaker instilled the values within all of his family members. She would spend hours with him, feed him, take him for walks in the woods, teaching the names of trees and flowers. His grandmother Salyer, on the other hand, had a *fire* about her. She had the same good heart of his grandmother Whitaker, but she would whip him in a minute. Tom recalls he once got a whipping for holding a towel too long against the end of his nose! One of her favorite expressions was "I'll scratch your eyes out!" Of course artists have detailed memories, and Tom remembers taking that warning literally.

With strength of values and fire of will, Tom believes his two grandmothers made the perfect pair. The Appalachian fiery spirit, Tom believes, goes all the way back to the Civil War. He wondered why his family did not get along with some of the other families on the creek and came to find out that the ancestors of these folks fought on the other side in the Civil War. Tom is proud of *all* his influences.

On his visit to my class, Tom brought two very different paintings to illustrate two worlds within Appalachia. One was the home place of a man he knew who lived to be 102 years old. He and his sister lived side by side, having themselves married brother and sister. They had many children who became double first cousins—as many as 25 to 30. When Pap was 96, his sister died. He was asked about missing her. After all, they had played together as children and watched each other's children grow into adulthood with children of their own. His words were simply, "I ain't got no time to worry about what's going on around me." This statement is not as callous as it might appear on the surface, for here was a man who loved and appreciated life so intensely that he had no time for grieving over a loss.

The other painting Tom brought to class was of the Mayo

mansion on Third Street in Paintsville, Kentucky. When I was growing up, this mansion was the home of Our Lady of the Mountains Catholic School. I had known a few children who had attended school there and had accepted the nuns who passed me on the sidewalks of town as part of my community although I knew little about the Catholic faith. To Tom the painting of the mansion represented another world seldom portrayed—a world of wealth and grandeur—the world of coal barons like John C. C. Mayo, who prospered in the mountains by purchasing mineral rights from our forefathers.

Tom stressed the importance of drawing representations of both worlds in Appalachia, but when he asked my students, "Which world do you think means the most to me?" He gave his usual characteristic pause for thought on their part and then said, "Hell, I grew up sleeping in a wood house, not a brick one, with no wallpaper on the walls, and I would wake up to find snow on the quilt! This one (Pap's place) means more to *me*. I know *both* worlds and associate with people in both, but I see beauty in the world I grew up in. I have not left it behind in exchange for the world represented by the Mayo mansion."

From behind the desk Tom lifted another painting that he had brought. This one was titled *Baptism*. Students always enjoy a piece of writing or art even more if they are given a story, one that they may recall whenever they read the piece again or see the painting hanging on an unfamiliar wall. In the case of a writer, the story may illustrate the reason for a poem's creation.

Tom began telling the story about *Baptism* by saying that he had not been to church in a year and a half. He was on his way one Sunday morning to the flea market. He heard a voice inside telling him to turn around and go to the church where his father was preaching.

"We all hear those unspoken voices from time to time, but I think some of us deny it," Tom said. He turned his car around and went back to the church. At the end of the regular service, his father baptized a lady from Royalton. Tom had his camera with him as usual and took pictures of the outdoor baptism that became the basis of his painting. His father died within a week.

Tom said that he painted it to "help deal with the death of my father." Many students could relate because they had used writing or art to help heal the pain of tragedies in their own lives. Painting *Baptism* was therapy for a grieving son.

Tom ended his presentation with a song he had written about a baptism, "There's Going to Be a Baptism Here Today." It was the first time he had ever sung the song in a class at Big Sandy Community and Technical College. By the time he finished, all were clapping, and even a few hallelujahs could be heard coming from the group.

Even though it had a fast-paced rhythm, the song had a touch of sadness, and Tom said he was once asked why so many mountain songs are sad. His response was, "You learn through sadness and struggle. Our ancestors knew that. You did the work first. Once the work or struggle was over, then came the time for relaxation and pleasure." Our music and singing were sad but also cathartic. Singing a sad song was like doing the work first. It got the sadness out of your system and cleared the way for enjoyment and peace. For this same reason mountain Bluegrass music is more popular than ever today.

Tom J. Whitaker best understands and paints the beauty and sadness of his *first* world—a world he never really left behind. Tom still has a *feeling* for the simple way of life he has preserved through the beauty of his art.

CHAPTER TWELVE

Although some excellent, qualified teachers in the mountains taught me many lessons, none taught me to appreciate the culture of my people. In the fifties and sixties in the mountains of east Kentucky and elsewhere in our nation the idea of respect for diversity had not become popular as it is today. This was the era of segregated schools in Kentucky, but even if schools had been integrated, I would have had no classes with African Americans because none lived in Johnson County. I was taught to be humble and never to think of myself as being better than anyone else on any basis, so I did not understand the mistreatment of African Americans. I heard about Malcolm X and Martin Luther King, Jr., but I did not fully understand the history of the African American culture. If I had known more about the heritage and history of African Americans, I would have found many similarities between their story and the story of my people. Both experienced transplantation in the form of great migrations toward northern cities in search of jobs. Both African Americans and Appalachians suffered degradation from those materially advantaged who thought of themselves as being superior. *Hillbilly* was/is the word used to stereotype and make fun of east Kentuckians much the same as the word *nigger* was used to portray African Americans as inferior to whites.

In the sixties African Americans rebelled against assimilation of another's cultural beliefs. They began to take pride in their differences and in the history and accomplishments of their ancestors who had survived or escaped slavery. Our teachers in the mountains thought they could best do their jobs by *saving* us from our heritage. We were not taught our history. They seemed to buy in to the *hillbilly* stereotype themselves and felt obligated to teach us to deny our heritage and learn to talk like Chet Huntley and David Brinkley on NBC's flagship news program from 1956 through 1970, the Huntley-Brinkley Report. WSAZ's NBC affiliate in Huntington, West Virginia was one of the most powerful stations at the time and the television station of choice for residents of the Big Sandy Valley. A road in Martin County was even named the *Huntley-Brinkley* Highway in thanks for a report done on their nightly newscast about the need for the road's construction. When you are taught to imitate the language of newscasters and to assimilate someone else's culture, you have to assume there is something inferior about your own language and culture.

Our teachers in the sixties zealously took it upon themselves to change our way of talking. Dianne Stambaugh was a classmate of mine at Flat Gap in third grade. Although her grandparents were farmers and miners like my own, Dianne's parents, unlike my own, had never lived anywhere else than their holler. My mother had been quick to adopt some of the accent of her Dayton, Ohio neighbors. I suppose she thought these people superior because they had more material possessions than she. I'm sure some of my teachers felt the same way and so did their best to make sure we imitated our northern neighbors. I modeled my mother's way of speaking more than my grandparents'; however, listening to Dianne was like listening to our grandparents seated beside us. She would ask, "Is *hit* about time for recess?" Our teacher winced upon hearing the word, and although she corrected Dianne with kindness, Dianne was still made to feel ashamed of the way her grandparents and she talked. Teachers were not trained to build self-esteem. Heritage was something taught in history classes, and our nation's heritage was the topic. Lessons about that heritage included very little about Appalachians. Our parents drove within one hundred feet every day of "Blockhouse Bottom," where Harmon Station, Kentucky's first permanent fort, was established, yet we were not taught about our history and our heritage. Our teachers' mission was to teach us to write and speak like "educated" people. They could not have realized that Dianne hurt inside. Her lesson and ours was that our grandparents and we were inferior. Our language is who we are. The first step in teaching students to abandon their heritage is to tell them the language of their grandparents is ignorant. Dianne should have been taught the beauty of her language as the purest reflection of her culture.

The first premonition I had that I might work with language and become a writer some day came while I was sitting on the gray, wooden porch steps of my Slone grandparents' home, watching and listening as my father cut my grandfather's hair. I did not reflect on this demonstration of my father's love for my papaw at the time, but what I perceived as a child was preparation for my writing although I had no realization of that at the time. I just recall thinking that I had mentally recorded a moment that would never leave me.

I was always the quiet one. I must have seemed a tad suspicious to my relatives—like a spy listening intently to conversations in which they could not imagine a child taking any interest. I did not begin writing until I was forty-four. When I began, my writing came on me fast and strong as if a floodgate had been opened. All my life I had been unconsciously *absorbing* what was going on around me.

I have always noticed details without understanding why. I remember, for example, the headlines of news stories on wallpaper, pasted on the walls of a deserted house I was not supposed to enter but did. (My grandparents knew one who had lived there had died with tuberculosis, and they carried the fear of this disease with them—the same fear that had been passed through the generations back to our European ancestors.) Today I realize, as I did not when I was younger, how important it is to be always open to possible new subjects for my writing. Jesse Stuart carried with him always slips of paper and a pencil in order to capture the details of his life and the lives of those he observed. He was constantly on the lookout for bits and pieces of life and language to put into his writing. James Still wrote in his *Wolfpen Notebooks*, originally spiral-bound notebooks, unique sayings, descriptive phrases, and unusual syntaxes. He loved to hear the language of his Knott County neighbors and recorded what he heard honestly with no feeling that his own language was superior.

Young people today do not take the time to pay attention to their surroundings. I rarely meet young people on my walks in the hemlock woods near Paintsville Lake. Oh, I see small children who walk because their parents insist, but once young people are in their teens when the choice is their own, they prefer cruising in cars, playing video and computer games, or watching movies and TV to slow walks in the woods. I am not sad because they are missing out on details they might some day put into writing, for few will write seriously except to earn a grade or secure a promotion. I am sad because they are missing out on the richness of the experience of living.

I believe many Appalachians pass through the same stages of acceptance of culture that I did. I resisted my teachers' attempts at *cleansing* me of my culture. I spent a considerable amount of time paying respect to other cultures while ignoring my own. One of my favorite graduate school professors in Xavier University's English department was Dr. Ernie Fontana. He was a wonderful, competent teacher of James Joyce and Joseph Conrad. His modern British literature classes were always filled to capacity. He was an animated teacher who possessed an obvious wealth of knowledge of subject along with an intense passion for literature which had become a very part of him. I have forgiven Dr. Fontana for forcing me to read Thomas Hardy's poetry aloud in class: "Let us hear that mountain accent as you read for us." I may have imitated my mother's acquired Dayton accent, but my grandparents' influence was still present in the way I talked. I felt ashamed and wanted to lose what was left of the traditional way my grandparents spoke but could not manage to do so. I read as he asked me to, but I did not read with *pride*. Dr. Fontana did not intend to embarrass me. He simply enjoyed hearing an accent different from the one he heard daily. Perhaps it even made Hardy's poems sound more authentic, for his people were rural people from Wessex, England.

I knew that I wanted to teach like Dr. Fontana some day. In order to do so, I would have to discover content that I too was passionate about. I would need to discover literature that I too could internalize. I have made that discovery in the works of Kentucky and Appalachian writers. I am sitting beside Jim Wayne Miller on the torn bench seat of that old pick-up truck parked beside the French Broad River. We are listening to Bluegrass together as the "white doves" of our troubles fly from our chests. I am walking with Wendell Berry on his Kentucky River farm as he considers his Port William membership in *his* Kentucky community. I am sitting in a ladder-backed, cane-bottom chair under the shade of a sycamore tree with

James Still listening and agreeing as he explains he is "of Kentucky."

I introduce my students to writers such as Jesse Stuart, Billy C. Clark, James Still, Jim Wayne Miller, Wendell Berry, and Silas House on five campuses throughout the southern Big Sandy Valley from Paintsville to Pikeville. I teach writing and Appalachian literature on the Prestonsburg campus of Big Sandy Community and Technical College in our new Postsecondary Center for Education, a state-of-the-art facility that we share with Morehead State University. Students can enroll in two Appalachian literature courses, HUM 202 and HUM 204. These courses help fulfill general studies requirements toward four-year undergraduate degrees. Once students complete a block of transfer courses, they may continue pursuing their bachelor's degree at MSU without leaving their hometowns and without the expense of doing so.

Sometimes I teach on four campuses: Prestonsburg, Prestonsburg High School, Johnson Central High School, and Mayo Technical College in Paintsville. College classes on high school campuses provide gifted students the opportunity to enter college full-time with college credits already completed. They provide an effective transition into college-level work for students who have almost completed their high school credits. Many students enrolled in my high school campus classes have recently completed a summer of college life while participating in the Governor's Scholar program on the campus of Centre College in Danville, Eastern Kentucky University in Richmond, or Bellarmine College in Louisville. They are anxious to continue their college experiences. Teaching older non-traditional students is rewarding, but so is teaching these young people, ages seventeen or eighteen. They rejuvenate this thirty-year educator.

Imagine the thrill of being able to introduce these students to the writing of Linda Scott DeRosier! Her memoir *Creeeker—A Woman's Journey* is about growing up in Johnson County. Students go home and talk to their parents and grandparents about what life and work and the role of women was like in the mountains in the fifties and sixties. They are able to reflect on changes and decide for themselves which changes are for the better and which are not. They discover how connected the writer was/is to her *place* and compare her attachment to place to that of other Kentucky writers. They discover the make-up of the community from which Linda DeRosier came and consider whether there is still a sense of community in Kentucky as reflected in the modern works of writers like Silas House, Crystal Wilkinson, and Frank X. Walker.

College classes offered in Paintsville make a college degree even more accessible to students from Johnson, Lawrence, and Martin counties who have a shorter drive to Paintsville than to Prestonsburg in order to attend classes. They provide rich teaching experiences for me as well: the Lawrence County student whose mother worked for Ricky Skagg's mother Dorothy and who knows people who still remember the Lawrence County writer and educator, Dr. Cratis Williams; the underground coal miner who packed up his Bronco II with all his belongings and drove to Florida to work as a deck hand on a deep sea fishing boat; or Casey, my Van Lear student who was raised by her grandparents up Pea Vine (also known as Schoolhouse Holler) a short distance from Loretta Lynn's Butcher Holler homeplace. Her papaw wore "dark-rimmed glasses that slid down his nose at least twenty times a day." His clothing never stopped with one layer: "Papaw always thought you'd catch cold if the wind blew in your favor. Under his bibs he wore a white Hanes tee shirt, sometimes with a white "A" undershirt below that. It was not uncommon to find a pair of worn long johns covering his legs and two pairs of socks, followed by a pair of old miners' work pants with cigarette holes in them from the Camels he smoked." He was a retired coal miner of forty years who drove two hours each way to work each day, crawled around in knee-high coal ten to twelve hours a day just to drive two hours back home and start all over again. But when Casey was a little girl in her papaw's life, "He had all the time in the world for this little girl who needed him." Together they would visit the Paintsville Stockyard flea market every Saturday morning. Casey remembered the white bunny she begged for that her papaw bought for her. While chasing it under a couch, she pulled off its tail. Her mamaw told her, no— she could not sew the rabbit's tail back on, so her papaw drove her to a garden near Loretta Lynn's home and convinced her that if they "planted" the tail and set the bunny free, the tail would grow a new rabbit. She knew her papaw would never lie.

James Still rode horseback or walked from one-room school to one-room school carrying books to students. He would take a box of books to one school, exchange it for a box of books these students had read, and then take those books to another school. I do something similar today. My job is easier though, for I only need take along one copy of a book by a Kentucky writer, pass it around the classroom so that students can copy the title, author, and ISBN. Later they can visit a local bookstore to request a copy. If they are not certain they want to purchase the book, they can visit their town's public library or the college library and obtain the book on interlibrary loan even if that particular library does not have the book on its shelf.

I carry writing models between campuses as well as books. Today, for example, one paper written by Summer Blevins, my Johnson Central student, will be read and reviewed on the campus of Prestonsburg High as well as at Mayo Technical College in

Paintsville. Tomorrow I will read it for my students on our Prestonsburg campus. Students who drive to Prestonsburg for classes from as far away as Elkhorn City in extreme southern Pike County near the Virginia border will hear Summer's story about her "Pop" (grandfather) and about his snow-white hankie that becomes a symbol for the purity of his love for her and for his wife of forty-nine years. When he would lift Summer into his arms to give her a hug or to walk with her until she fell asleep, she would peek over her grandfather's shoulder and down his back to see his snow-white hankie dangling from his back pocket. Before his death her grandfather left instructions with Summer's grandmother to hand out eleven of his hankies to his loved ones as his way of being with them after his death. That reminder of his love rests on the front seat of Summer's car beside her as she drives to school each morning. Hopefully students on several campuses will listen and relate and perhaps even learn to *imitate* the beautiful details, symbolism, and comparisons in Summer's descriptive paper.

I am pleased and surprised when I introduce students to Kentucky or Appalachian writers, and they in turn introduce the writers to their family and friends. Often our college bookstore sells out of books I require for my classes such as James Still's *From the Mountain From the Valley* or Silas House's *Clay's Quilt*. Bookstores in Paintsville, Van Lear, Prestonsburg, and Pikeville soon become aware of popular titles and stock these books as well. The demand is largely created by word of mouth. One student introduces a book to a family member who in turn purchases the book as a gift for a relative who lives in another state. I am most pleased when I hear something like what I heard when I did a book signing recently in Huntington, West Virginia, at the Ohio River Valley Festival of Books. One of the festival organizers came up to Joe Survant, Kentucky's poet laureate and explained that his was the first poetry book that he had read all the way through. I often hear my students say that a book by a Kentucky writer was left on a coffee table only to be picked up and read by a family member who had not read a book in years. It is common for me to see two bookmarks in books my students bring to class for class discussion. One marks the place for a mother or a father who is also reading the book. Staff and faculty on our campuses borrow my books. I never worry about whether they will be returned. A staff member who works in our college bookstore borrowed Verna Mae Slone's *How We Talked* and recently returned it to tell me how much she had enjoyed reading it. Mrs. Slone enjoyed reading college books her children were using in their classes—those she was interested in. She should be proud to know that her *What My Heart Wants To Tell* is one of the most popular books my students share with family and friends. I like to think that I am introducing books to hundreds just as Mr. Still did.

Chapter Thirteen

My years at Eastern Kentucky University were formative ones that made all the difference in my life. I met my wife Debbie there. I met people from all across our state and in fact all over the world. During my junior year my roommate was Peter Yen Wai Ming, a native of Hong Kong. We were alike and different in so many ways. He drove a rusted, lime green Ford Mustang that reminded me of my first $250 car. He had a job to help pay his way through school as did I. He worked at Bundy, a Winchester factory, making belts and hoses for automobiles. He owned only one coat the same as I, and we both loved to complain about the biting winter winds in Richmond. I would turn the key and open the door to my dorm room in Commonwealth Hall to the smell of boiled chicken with Chinese curd. His desk shelves were stocked with curd and spices, and dried vegetables that he had bought in New York City's Chinatown upon his arrival in the United States. We were not allowed to cook in our dorm rooms, but most of us did anyway because cooking saved money. After I earned the Modern Language Scholarship, I could afford to eat out but only once a day, and to purchase a meal plan would have taken all my extra money away. I suspect that Peter saved his extra money or wired it home to family. He had a group of Asian friends on campus who spoke Cantonese when they would visit. I remember feeling uncomfortable because of course I did not understand a single word. Peter's English was difficult for *me* to understand at first—especially when we talked on the phone. In person we soon had no trouble at all communicating. I learned a great deal about his native Hong Kong, and he learned a great deal about the mountains of east Kentucky.

One conversation I recall revealed the sense of community he and his family felt while living in one of the most overpopulated cities in the world. He explained that he and his family lived in a small apartment in a high-rise building. The ratio of police officers to the rest of the population was much smaller than in Kentucky. Residents knew that if there was trouble nearby, they must take it upon themselves to become a citizen police force. He remembered his father picking up a club he kept for just such a purpose and, accompanied by friends and neighbors, rushing out into the street to help someone who was being attacked and robbed. I was not very far removed from a time in the mountains when the community would come to the aid of a neighbor. I imagined that my grandfather had done much the same at a time when the local sheriff was miles of bad roads away in Paintsville.

Peter even offered advice—one culture to another. I was dating my future wife Debbie who is two years older than I. He said in Hong Kong the man never marries an older woman. When I asked why, he only replied, "They will be *smarter* than you." I did not understand the relationship of age to wisdom and did not listen to his advice. Debbie and I married less than a year after my graduation. Peter was correct! She *is* smarter than I am, but I still fail to see what age has to do with it.

Peter listened to my mountain stories as I listened to his stories of growing up in his native Hong Kong. He even learned to enjoy the cornbread and soup beans my mother would send with me in a "care" package back to college when I would return from a weekend visit home to the mountains. I never developed a taste for his cooked chicken with curd over rice though.

Just because I have spent the majority of my teaching career in the mountains does not mean I have missed out on the opportunity to teach foreign students. One way to teach students to value their cultural identity is to show them a culture completely different from their own. One student of mine, Victa Parsa, came to Big Sandy Community and Technical College having already earned a graduate degree from Teheran University in Iran. She was taking my writing class for a very practical reason. She needed to learn how to express herself using correct English grammar and syntax so that she could pass the admissions test and be successful in her personal interview in order to gain admittance to the University of Kentucky's School of Pharmacy.

She had learned of my use of model writers and the peer review process through her husband who teaches math at my college. She had been in this country less than a year, and although she had studied English in Iran, she had done so as many Americans study a foreign language, never considering that some day they might actually have to *use* it in their careers. She felt that by listening to American students read their papers and by reading Kentucky writers, she would more quickly learn the grammar she needed.

Victa's father had been a medical doctor in Iran. Inspired by his example, she had trained to be a midwife. In one of her papers, she wrote about the friendship between her father and a famous Iranian author of children's books. She recalled the thrill she felt when her father had brought home to her a book with the author's signature and a personal message written especially for her.

The central character of one of her favorite stories written by the author was a tiny fish who spent its life dreaming of the sea and wondering what it would be like to swim there. He had spent his life swimming in what we in the mountains would call a branch, but loved to dream of being in the ocean.

One evening after work, Victa's father returned home with news that the author had been killed. When she was older, she understood why the writer had been killed. Besides his children's stories, he had also written in protest of his government's restrictive social and political policies. He had been murdered to silence his pen.

When she read the parable to my class, my students realized she had a gift for writing narratives. She compared the writer to his character, the tiny fish. Both longed to see the ocean—symbol of creative and political freedom. She wrote in her closing that in death the writer was strolling along the beach, breathing the salt air, feeling the wind-blown salt against his skin as he stared off into the infinity of the horizon—finally free.

It must be understood, I did not allow Victa to read her story in my class until I had read an early draft with her and suggested corrections that would put the piece into standard English. For most of my students this revision can be done on a lab (individual help) day when I can sit beside them and help them see needed improvements. I accompanied Victa to a computer lab where I could help her to revise each sentence into correct English grammar.

Victa was so proud when she read her corrected paper aloud and found students enjoyed hearing her writing. As her confidence grew, so did her skills. She did not realize initially that she was also helping me *teach*. Her depiction of her culture taught my students the value of acknowledging and accepting cultural differences everywhere.

Of course Victa was not proud of every part of her culture. Just as in east Kentucky, much of what there is to be ashamed of has always come from the politics, which often do little to improve social and living conditions. East Kentucky students can relate. Promises, whether federal (the 60's war on poverty) or local, are rarely kept here as in her home country.

Another story Victa shared through her writing illustrated cultural similarities between her home and east Kentucky. It was about a special professor at her university in Iran. When he entered the classroom, all students would stand out of respect for his knowledge and training. They appreciated that he was willing to come to their campus to teach them.

Writers should take the reader along with them into the setting of their stories. As she read, we all felt as if we too were standing out of respect for our professor. We could see his silver hair, so long it was combed back, and his silver-framed half glasses resting near the tip of his nose. He wore a dark tie under the starched collar of his white shirt. We could see our reflections in the lenses of his glasses as we took our seats preparing ourselves to take lecture notes. This day something was different though. Her professor had brought to class and placed on top of his leather briefcase a long stemmed yellow rose. He explained that the university usually sent a car to pick him up, but on this day the driver had arrived fifteen minutes late. Even though they were late, he had the driver stop a moment at a street vendor's stand so that he could purchase the yellow rose. He had brought it as a gift to his class to apologize to them for being late.

I watched for my non-traditional students' facial expressions and could see they understood why Victa had remembered this story in such vivid detail. The respect she had for her teacher had been returned in kind. Mutual respect was and is the foundation for education whether in Iran or in east Kentucky.

Pronouncing the surnames of students is a skill not taught in college education courses. I remember that moment of panic when I first attempted to pronounce the last names of my northern Kentucky students. Specific regions of Kentucky were settled at different times through different migration routes, and so the sets of surnames in each part of the state vary. I never met a Craig in east Kentucky, but in northern Kentucky Craigs abound. I never taught a Wheeler or a Slone in northern Kentucky, but I have yet to attend a commencement ceremony for Big Sandy Community and Technical College when I fail to hear a Slone or Wheeler's name called as she or he proudly crosses the stage to receive a diploma. Several of our most uncomfortable graduation ceremonies were made so by virtue of our college president who was from north of Dallas, Texas, and our dean of students who was from another part of the state attempting in vain to pronounce east Kentucky surnames correctly. My son, Stephen, was a presidential ambassador at Northern Kentucky University where he was often called upon to stand beside their president, Dr. Votruba, also a non-native Kentuckian, so that he could help him pronounce the names of scholarship recipients. Whether receiving scholarships or diplomas or simply being recognized as being in attendance, students want to hear their names pronounced correctly. Learning how to do so in an area where you did not grow up takes a while and comes with many slip-ups along the way.

College teachers meet students from all over the country and the world in their classes and seem always a little more prepared for the challenge of learning to pronounce new names than their secondary school counterparts. One fall semester I saw the name *Espy* on my Spanish class roster. The name was unusual enough, but what made it even more so was that it was followed by a common Kentucky surname—Taylor. I came to learn that Espy, a non-traditional student and resident of Johnson County, had grown up in Mexico speaking Spanish, but she had received little education there. She had never learned to read or write Spanish well. Here was an English literate, Spanish *illiterate* student who had enrolled in my class to learn to read and write her native language.

Espy's father had moved his family to this country so that he could earn a better living. She had learned to read and write English on her own and had passed the GED exam, thereby earning the opportunity to enroll in college. She and her American husband had settled in east Kentucky after vacationing through the state one summer. Her husband found a job in the coal business during the coal boom of the late seventies, and they had raised their children in Johnson County and so considered it their home.

The *most* unusual thing about Espy's name was the fact that it was derived from the Hispanic name *Esperanza* (a-spa-rahn-sah) which in Spanish means *hope*. Espy loved her name as she did her Hispanic culture, but she had given up *hope* that anyone in east Kentucky other than Spanish teachers would learn to pronounce it correctly, so she had settled for an abbreviated version. I will never have a more willing and eager student than she.

Another student without an east Kentucky surname appeared in my writing class in the fall of 2002. Candy Tubin's name was not as unusual as her story. When I saw her that first day of class, I knew she looked familiar to me although certainly foreign amongst east Kentucky students. I had seen her and her family often at Paintsville Lake State Park. Her physician husband had a boat that he trailered to the lake. She had long, straight dark hair and a dark Hawaiian complexion. Her eyes were Asian. She spoke softly with short simple sentences accentuated with hand movements. In her first paper she described her initial impressions of our country. Louisville, Kentucky, was the first American city she visited. Her Brazilian-born fiancé was finishing his medical training at the University of Louisville School of Medicine. Her flight landed at Louisville's Standiford Field in December. Her first impression was inspired, as she looked through the window of the plane at all the barren trees in neighborhoods surrounding the airport. She had never known seasons before in her native Philippines, so she thought that the trees were dead. Her fiancé explained to her that deciduous trees lose their leaves in winter.

Candy described growing up in the Philippines. One particular detail that stood out for east Kentucky students listening as she read her paper was the poverty she had experienced. My students had heard similar stories from their parents or grandparents. Her home had no running water, so she and her sisters had carried water in pails tied to a long wooden pole, which rested to balance the pails on their shoulders. Carrying water from a stream to wash clothes was once common in the mountains of east Kentucky.

The straw baskets her family made by hand would be taken to an open-air market to be sold. My students thought of the Paintsville Stock Market (flea market) where their own relatives set up booths to sell hand-made items. In her last few paragraphs, Candy described her life in America with her new husband, now a practicing physician.

In another paper, Candy described how she felt the first time she ate in a Louisville restaurant, her fiancé's favorite—Outback Steak House. When the steaks arrived, she looked down on hers with an anxious smile. At home she had not eaten steaks such as these, and as she took her first cut into the meat, she was shocked to see red liquid oozing from inside. Never before had she eaten a medium-rare piece of meat, but she wanted to make the effort because she knew her Brazilian-born fiancé preferred his steak cooked this way. Each bite brought on more nausea, but she struggled through as many bites as she could. This was not the only culture clash during the meal. As her fiancé chewed his tossed salad, she had flashbacks of cattle grazing on fresh leaves of grass. Until then, she had never seen a man eat *uncooked* greens. There was no such thing as raw salad in her country except as food for the cows.

Another of her papers told of the accident she had while driving in an east Kentucky snow. On her island she had ridden on bicycles and in motor scooter sidecars, but she had never driven an automobile until she arrived in Kentucky. The accident could have badly injured her, for her Ford Explorer turned over several times, completely caving in its roof. She said that her family saw the vehicle before they arrived at the hospital to see her, and they were certain that she had died. She escaped with only a cut on her head. Candy was less than four feet eight and had complained all her life about being short, but she would never complain again. Her size saved her life.

Together Candy and her husband had visited most American cities, discovering something unique and wonderful about each one. She inspired my students to want to visit them too when they were on their own with their degrees behind them. Candy ended her first paper with the words, "God Bless America." She was showing my students that she had become an American, and that immigrants filled with the ambition to succeed should still be welcomed here.

It became clear to my students that Candy could teach them about a very different culture they might otherwise never learn about from a book. They "adopted" her. They took care of her. For example, when they were ready to read their papers aloud in class for peer review and editing suggestions, they would make a special effort to have an extra copy of their papers to hand to her. They instinctively knew that someone new to our region would need help in order to understand our colloquialisms.

One of the first struggles Candy had with English was learning to use prepositions correctly. She would choose the wrong one and so express the wrong relationship between her ideas. She would not understand the small shade of difference in meaning between the prepositions, *on* and *in* for example. By the end of the semester, Candy made fewer errors because she had the opportunity to read and hear other papers and receive help from her classmates and from the professor.

The last paper written in our class was a process assignment. Students were encouraged to bring an example of a process they knew how to do well to accompany their papers as they read them aloud. One non-traditional student brought teaching materials for kindergarten and first-grade students so that she could demonstrate some of her favorite children's learning activities. She was working in the America Reads program as a tutor and teacher's aide. Her dream was to become an elementary teacher, and her love for children was apparent as she showed the class her techniques and materials. When we asked where the money came from to purchase rewards and games for her students, she said she spent her own money. Good teachers don't wait for supplies that may or may not arrive. They find school supply stores or catalogs and purchase their own. Those in class with parents who were teachers immediately recognized one who had chosen the correct career path for herself.

Another non-traditional student, Raymond Horn, who loved to fish in bass tournaments, brought to class his rods, reels, and tackle. He demonstrated casting techniques and bait retrieval methods. Even novice fishermen benefited from his paper and his demonstration. His passion for tournament fishing was infectious.

Another young man wrote about his passion—singing. He had recently sung for the dedication of a new building on our campus, so we knew something of his talent. He wrote about the hours of practice involved in perfecting a song, and he described his nerves and shaking legs as he performed for the first time in front of his peers, friends, and family members under the lights on the stage of the Mountain Arts Center. We could not see how nervous he was in the videotape he brought to share with us, but we could hear his obvious talent. Everyone in class agreed that he had a gift. He was too humble about his talent. Reading his paper and showing us his performance removed a layer of insecurity and gave him confidence in his singing ability as well as his writing ability.

Candy's process paper was filled with cultural connections to the mountains of east Kentucky. Her topic was fashion. Upon arriving in the area, she was unable to find petite-size clothing in department stores. Relying on the skills she had learned when she was poor, she purchased a sewing machine and a few patterns, and set about sewing her own clothing. She was doing just as her mother and grandmother had taught her, but this time she was sewing not because she could not afford to purchase ready-made clothes but because they were not available. She discovered that the clothes she made ended up fitting and looking much better than clothes she saw in stores.

After she read her paper, she was pleased to find female students so interested. They too recalled their grandmothers making dresses from G. C. Murphy's five-and-ten-cent store patterns and material. Most were attending college while working as well and were interested in saving money wherever possible. Candy brought pictures of dresses she had made. She left the room to change into four outfits, putting on her own fashion show. They ranged from informal shorts to a sequined formal gown. (The materials from which the gown was sewn cost less than fifteen dollars at Wal-mart.) My students enjoyed her paper and her fashion show as well. Two cultures collided, and the result was that the similarities, not the differences, were important.

CHAPTER FOURTEEN

The importance of sharing the work of model writers with my students became clear to me early in my career when I was teaching English at Gallatin County High School. Most young teachers believe their students all want and value an education.

One opinionated student, upon being assigned an argumentation paper in English class, proceeded to give his paper the title "Who Needs English Teachers?" I was excited to receive it because the paper's weaknesses answered the question. *He* needed English teachers. The paper had errors of every imaginable type: incorrect subject-verb agreement to fragments, comma splices, misspelled possessives, etc. "What a wonderful irony!" I thought. I was thrilled to have an example paper I could use to demonstrate mistakes to

Johnson Building, Prestonsburg Community College, 1964.

students who would certainly see the embarrassment that similar writing errors in their own work could bring. I hurried into the copying room to duplicate the paper.

The next day as my first English class saw the paper, the reaction was not what I had expected. Students saw the errors, but the type of mistakes made by this particular student did not surprise them. Gallatin County High was a small enough school so that everyone knew each other. My students knew this student was waiting it out until his sixteenth birthday to drop out. They saw no reason to humiliate him in front of others. They corrected his errors because I asked them to, but they acted as if they were watching a guilty man being hung in a public square.

I would never again use a negative example paper in my classes. From that point on I have used model papers and works from model writers that inspire because of their excellence. I learned that I could not embarrass students into wanting to learn correct writing. My offices at home and at my college are filled with positive example papers. Each semester students who see the word *model* written at the top of their paper learn that I may use this particular piece of their writing to inspire similar writing by other students who may be struggling. Using model papers in this way provides a bonus. Students who have written model papers gain self-confidence.

I am convinced that the only way students learn to write correctly is by reading correct writing. It is the lack of reading today that results in poor writing skills. The more model papers students read the better their own writing becomes.

Published writers have themselves produced model pieces. When students read Crystal Wilkinson's short stories about her childhood experiences growing up in rural Casey County, they begin to model her by writing their own stories about gathering at their grandmothers' for Sunday dinners or listening to their grand-fathers' United Baptist sermons. Students enjoy reading models when they can relate to content. They love discovering Kentucky writers who write about ordinary parts of life they have taken for granted—a Kentucky writer whom they enjoy reading so much that they may go to the library or bookstore to find more titles by that author. I often find myself today responding to the question: "Where can I find this book for myself or for my children?" I tell them about local library collections and about booksellers like Joseph-Beth in Lexington, Words and Stuff in Van Lear, or the Jesse Stuart Foundation in Ashland.

Model papers have a way of showing up when needed. When I began using positive student models, I had only my own work as a student to share. One of the first model papers I used was a comparison/contrast paper written while I was a graduate student at Xavier University in Cincinnati. It was a literature paper about the similarities between Stephen Crane's short story "The Blue Hotel" and Joseph Conrad's "Heart of Darkness." It was the old type of literature paper that itself modeled professors' efforts to publish in literary journals such as the Modern Language Association's.

My students saw in my paper the latest MLA form of documentation. They saw that the old system of footnoting their high school teachers had taught them had been replaced with internal parenthetical documentation. They could relate little to the content, though, and could see no practical reason for searching for obscure points of literary comparison that might lead to some observation never before discovered by fellow English major researchers. I remember reading a similar college paper written by my high school English teacher. But I also remember appreciating that she would go out of her way to share an example from her own education that might help her students succeed in college themselves some day.

Soon I began receiving papers in my writing classes that could become models and inspire imitation. I could not wait to make copies to share with my students. One such paper rests in my office still today under a handmade doll with long, stringy blonde hair, yellow eyes to match, and skinny, long legs that dangle and weigh the rest of the doll's body down so that she cannot sit upright for long. Judy, the doll's maker, entered my classroom along with a typical group of community college students. Some were close to her nontraditional age with grown children of their own in college. Others were in their twenties, married, with a couple of years of minimum-wage jobs behind them, a baby, and a rent payment. Ginger Burns was from Carrollton, Kentucky. She had been injured in a car accident, was now a paraplegic and a patient receiving therapy at the Carl D. Perkins Rehabilitation Center in neighboring Johnson County. Others were traditional-aged college students who were working toward two-year degrees or were planning to transfer to Morehead State, Eastern Kentucky University, or Marshall in Huntington, West Virginia, in a year or two.

Judy wore dresses my mother would have worn had she been in my classes. Her long hair was always tied back. Her eyes were the unmistakable eyes of a reader—intelligent and determined. Through reading her diagnostic essay, I learned that her children were grown. One was a minister, and the other was a teacher. She had always loved reading. Her sons had nearly *forced* her into attending college. She had been reluctant because she believed she had been away from school so long that she would be slow in comparison to the younger students. Her sons had long ago recognized her potential—her gift—and had finally succeeded in cajoling their mother into enrolling in college.

What I will remember most about Judy is that I could never convince her that she had a gift for writing. Yes, she read her essays and stories aloud in my class as was required, but the volume of the applause never convinced her that she had talent. That applause came without my prompting, as students of all backgrounds recognized a gifted writer when they heard one. "Mary Ann" was the story of Judy's eighth birthday. Her paper began with a description of her chores on the farm, one of which was feeding chickens. She even described the sound of the feed as it was being poured into the feeding trough. What set her writing apart was its use of close detail that made the readers feel as if they were there sharing Judy's childhood experiences. She used an economy of words, still always evoking emotions as she recreated her memories.

Judy's mother kept house for a preacher. She described his tiny wire-rimmed glasses, which he used to look down his nose at her as he reached out his hand to give Judy some money for candy. This illustrated his feeling of superiority over Judy and her family. Then she projected in a daydream what it would be like to be the daughter of the owner of a candy store. She pictured a candy store proprietor's children with smiles displaying rotted teeth.

Just as the reader begins to feel sorry for the little girl and her poor east Kentucky family, Judy's focus shifts to the Mary Ann doll itself, for that is the birthday gift her mother gives to her. She unwraps the doll from white meat-wrapping paper, the same type of doll that sits slumped in my office today, with long stringy blonde hair, homemade calico dress, blue button eyes, and cloth shoes to match her hair at the end of long, limply dangling legs. Judy closed the true story of receiving the doll with, "Other little girls could have the Barbie doll she had been wishing for. She had Mary Ann.

Judy did not actually give me *her* Mary Ann doll from childhood. Instead she told me she made these dolls today as gifts; she never sold them. She knew I had a ten-year-old daughter and came to class one day with Mary Ann hidden in a used Wal-Mart bag. I accepted the doll but also the gift of her story about the doll to share with future students. "Mary Ann" now begins each of my semesters of college teaching as a model of what detailed, descriptive, papers can achieve. East Kentucky is a land of storytellers. Listening to stories has kept the story-telling tradition alive. Just as our ancestors modeled the story telling of their family members, students today need to read and hear stories and model story-telling tradition.

Stacy, another non-traditional student of mine, discovered the benefits of the Internet in a very personal way and wrote her own picture with words, describing the mixing together, not of the two worlds within Appalachian, but of England and Appalachia.

I first met Stacy when she entered my Appalachian literature class. She had three small children who loved hearing their mommy read to them at night. Her eyes lit up as I introduced my class to the children's writer, Cynthia Rylant and to her book, *When I Was Young in the Mountains*. Mountain children need to hear that their culture is worthwhile. In *When I Was Young in the* Mountains, Ms. Rylant delivers this lesson well. She closes the book with the words: "When I was young in the mountains, I never wanted to go to the desert, and I never wanted to go to the ocean, for I was in the mountains, and that was always enough." I always hand children's books to a female student so that she may read it aloud to her classmates thereby evoking students' memories of their mothers reading stories to them when they were small.

I know that fathers read to their children too as I did to my own two children, but I have no memory of my father reading to me— only my mother. She inspired in me a lifetime love of reading. A psychologist would say I am calling on a female reader so that I may return to my own childhood. Return to our childhoods we did as Stacy read to us, taking the time to hold the book above her head in order to show the beautiful illustrations. She read just as she had to her children the night before. Seeing a class of college students, some of whom are almost as old as I, engrossed in hearing a children's book read aloud is a wonderful thing—one of those times teachers dream about.

Stacy participated often and well in class because she enjoyed the Kentucky writers we were studying. She had worked ten years as a driver for Federal Express, making excellent money and earning job security, but she did not really like her job. She said that life is much too short to spend doing a job just for the money when you don't enjoy it. She had decided to become a teacher and, in addition to completing her course work, was practicing her skills by tutoring college students in our math lab.

Stacy had very specific goals typical of a non-traditional student. She knew the several math professors at Big Sandy Community and Technical College who were nearing retirement by *name*. This was one determined lady! She was going to continue beyond her bachelor's degree to earn a graduate degree so that she could become a colleague of her favorite math professor, Randy Watts. At least she wasn't going to college to replace *me*! I am convinced by her love for literature and her writing talent that she could if she chose to do so.

One day after class, Stacy brought a book to my desk. To my surprise it was the collection of poems done by the Lawrence County author, Dr. Francis Elam Burgess. I knew this copy was rare and had given up hope of ever finding one myself, but Stacy kindly let me borrow it. In a week or so, I received an e-mail. She said that her parents, after hearing about my interest in the writer, wanted me to keep the book. By giving the book to me, she and her family knew that I could share his poems with other students.

Another day after class, Stacy came by my office with a request for a return of the favor. She was entering an honorary society's scholarship competition and wanted my help to proofread a story she had written as a sample of her writing ability. As I read and helped her with little improvements that made her words flow more smoothly, I began to smile because I realized that this paper could be used as a model in my writing classes. Its topic was mature, and it carried readers along to a place they had probably never been.

Stacy had met her British husband through the Internet. Her paper was beautifully written, describing the old mill house that her future sister-in-law had restored where Stacy had shared her first meal with her future in-laws. Stacy described how out of place she felt in such a formal setting. The title of the paper "Pea'd Off" originated from the vegetable that was served. Stacy was in panic because she did not feel comfortable enough yet to totally be herself around her future British in-laws. She did not know the *proper* way to eat peas and felt as if she were participating in a cruel *test* to see whether she *measured up*. She alluded to the children's story "The Princess and the Pea," but she did not think of herself as the princess and was certain that she would fail the test.

Basing a story around such a simple act as eating peas may seem to be an unusual topic for a narrative, but in this case eating peas came to symbolize a clash of cultures. Stacy did what one would expect. She decided to postpone eating the peas while she watched others in order to learn the proper way. Her serving seemed to grow in size as it rested on her plate.

What Stacy's audience enjoyed was the way she described her

change from a person uncomfortable with who she was, where she was from, and what she had been taught into one who was secure enough in herself to eat the peas without caring about what others thought.

At the end of her story, Stacy decided to spoon the peas up as she had since she was a child and let others think what they pleased. But she did close the paper with the hope that she would never again have to eat peas.

CHAPTER FIFTEEN

I remember the old cliché often used as a theme in love songs, "If you love something, let it go in order to see whether it returns to you." I've discovered that this may not be always applicable to love, but it is certainly true of teaching writing. For the first fifteen years of my teaching career, I taught writing as writing had been taught to me. I stood and delivered, *lectured,* during the entire class period. As a young teacher I could not relinquish the control I felt by teaching this way. I still have folders filled with overhead transparencies holding models of every imaginable type of mechanical error found in grammar handbooks. I would stand or pace in front of the class like a mountain preacher filled with the spirit of the Word and monitor the ability of my students to copy the text examples and definitions from the screen.

I remember the experience of listening to my own voice while watching students quietly write down what was on the screen, but at the same time being aware that I was the *only* one in class listening. My students quickly learned that copying notes would get them by on quizzes or tests and that the real point of this activity was not to learn the process of writing but instead simply to learn to recite back to me what I had delivered to them.

I recall how irritated some students who copied notes more slowly than others would become when I pulled the transparency sheet away too soon. They understood, as I unfortunately at this time did not, that this game could be played well only if they copied notes quickly without listening to a single word I said. As a result, our only real communication with each other would come at times like these when students wanted me to slow down. One student in particular who took notes deliberately and slowly one day after class demanded that I make the notes available to her so that she could pass my test. After each class she would borrow my transparency sheets in order to make copies. I had no choice but to loan her the sheets. Otherwise I would have to move so slowly that faster writers would become even more bored.

No, faster note takers did not have to *become* bored in my classes. They were bored from the moment their pens first touched their notebooks. The boredom did seem to increase though when they would finish one sheet and grow steadily more and more impatient for me to move to another.

I cannot stress enough here, as much as it hurts to do so, that little or no communication about the writing process was actually going on. Oh, to a supervisor or to an administrator passing by my classroom, I *appeared* to be teaching, and the students seemed also to be quietly on task. But we were only participating in the process of recitation for the purpose of giving and receiving *grades*. I had learned a way to please my supervisors, and my students had learned a way to receive grades without bothering to engage in the learning process at all.

I am sorry to say that this style of teaching continued on my part much too long. Relinquishing control is not an easy task, but in the case of teaching writing, it is a necessary one. Perhaps the old cliché is valid after all—with a touch of revision: "If you love teaching and learning, let go of lecturing to see learning return."

In my experience *letting go* coincided with discovering Kentucky writers, using their works as models, and beginning to write myself. Letting go inspired in me the desire to replace lecture with a writing community. I discovered a practical way to build such a community in my classroom. The time it takes to do so is surprisingly short once the teacher *lets go* of the lecture method of delivery.

I begin each semester now with an emphasis on taking *pride* in writing. I bring to class a Wendell Berry poem titled "Do Not Be Ashamed." In this poem Mr. Berry insists that the reader hold on to the culture of his place and his people and never apologize for it, for to do so would be to abandon the truths his ancestors passed through the generations. Once we give up and "say we should be like them," we lose the pride and dignity that have been handed down to us from our grandparents and great grandparents. Students don't see the connection at first. I don't expect them to. But I do see through class discussion of the poem that they have always wanted a published writer to give them permission to be proud of their mountain culture. They are always surprised that Mr. Berry is not from east Kentucky, and perhaps at this point they are not ready to understand that Mr. Berry is talking about the importance of valuing the culture of a community anywhere in the world, not just in Henry County, Kentucky, or in their own east Kentucky mountains.

In a National Public Radio recorded interview, Mr. Berry is given an opportunity to read several of his poems from the collection *The Selected Poems of Wendell Berry*. I remember the excitement I felt upon discovering Wendell Berry's poems. As I introduce students to his writing, they can see that I *enjoy* reading the poems and that these poems have entered me—have become a part of me.

It is also important for students to hear Mr. Berry read his poems. Today teachers can easily access interviews with writers who read selections from their own work on line in the NPR archives. They can record the streaming of the interview on any format they wish and play it back for students, pausing for discussion of poems read or comments made about writing.

Mr. Berry reads his favorite poem written for his wife Tanya, "The Wild Rose." In it he writes that he would choose her again if given the chance. Re-discovering her as one might re-discover the beauty of a wild rose that had gone unnoticed before is his point in this poem. Wives in class who have recently felt unnoticed immediately identify with the central metaphor. Eighteen-year-old students who have never heard a metaphor applied to the relationship between a husband and wife begin to learn that comparisons can come from everyday life experience and relationships.

Most importantly students hear Mr. Berry read his own writing with *pride*. He reads slowly with careful emphasis on each word. There is beauty in the sound and rhythm of his language. It is clear he once made conscious choices about the words used to convey his relationship with his wife. No one could read these words as well as he because they are the result of his personal choices. He *owns* the words and their positioning in relation to one another.

I require that students read their papers *aloud*. When they first learn this, they are confused because they have heard other students say they enjoyed the class. They have often never read a paper in front of a group before. If they have done so, it was usually in a small group of four or five students who were never really serious about helping each other with their writing.

Once my students begin to see the value of their culture, they listen closely as I introduce them to writers who write about east Kentucky. Perhaps they have listened to family members who are storytellers in much the same vein as writers, Billy C. Clark, Silas House, and one of the first native east Kentucky voices, Jesse Stuart.

Jesse Stuart loved the spoken and the written word. Mr. Stuart was first and foremost a *teacher* himself. Even when he was writing, he was teaching. As I began thinking about this project, I re-read Jesse Stuart's classic, *The Thread That Runs So True*. When I first read that book, I had not yet taught a single class. I remember being jealous of the pride Mr. Stuart felt about his teaching as well as the pride he was able to inspire in his students. He never let his students use the excuse that they were from a small, poor school. They excelled in academic competitions with larger city schools. I came home to the mountains to teach in 1984—the same year Jesse Stuart died—and began rediscovering his writing shortly after I was hired at my college. In November of 2000, one of my students, Scott Justice, interviewed Jessica Adams, a native of Huntington, West Virginia, whose family were close friends of Jesse Stuart. My current students love to listen to Jessica's memories of Mr. Stuart and especially enjoy hearing about his writing habits and his love for the mountains.

Jessica's great uncle, Ben Webb, who was like a grandfather to her, was football coach at McHale High School in South Shore, Kentucky, when Jesse Stuart was principal there. They traveled together often. Ben's wife Jean and Jesse's wife Naomi Deane became close friends. Jesse met Jessica's grandfather through Ben. They became friends also. Although his name was Delmar, when he appears in Stuart's stories as the wealthy electrician in town, he is referred to as Del. Jessica's grandparents were with Jesse and his wife eating at a restaurant when Jesse had a heart attack. Delmar did CPR and saved the writer's life.

Jesse Stuart's high regard for Ben Webb was in part because

Ben was the first in his family to go to college. Those of my students who are first generation college students hear this and realize that they too deserve praise. At Ben's funeral, Jesse Stuart read a poem about his friend. In the poem Jesse expressed just how much he admired Ben as an educator. *The Thread That Runs So True* includes several of Jessica's family members, and they were proud to have been mentioned in Mr. Stuart's book.

Jessica's mom was a teacher, one of so many east Kentucky teachers influenced by Jesse Stuart's writing. She loves to remember what Jesse and Naomi Deane's home was like in W-Hollow in Greenup County. The inside of the home was filled with mementos from their travels. She remembered all the "knick knacks" from all over the world obtained during their many travels, but she also remembered note pads or slips of paper and pencils scattered throughout the home in case Jesse came up with an idea for his writing. Jessica's mom recalled that there was no TV in the home. Jesse and Naomi Deane had made the decision not to purchase a TV in large part because of the influence it might have upon their daughter Jane. Naomi Deane always nicely decorated the home for dinner parties because Jesse and she loved people and loved having company. According to Jessica's family, Naomi Deane was the perfect wife for Jesse. She was always taking care of him. She was as devoted to caring for him as in later years her daughter would be in caring for her.

Jessica's mom told her that Jesse and Naomi Deane were often the last to obtain modern conveniences because Jesse preferred that their lives remain as simple as possible. Once again today's non-traditional students can relate. Many have children and despair at the effect TV, video games, and technology have on them. Many have considered simplifying their own lives.

On the way to speaking engagements, Jessica's uncle Ben often drove the car for Jesse. He would look over to see Jesse looking out the window, busy writing down descriptions and ideas for his writing. He was always looking for ideas. Students discover that this is what separates writers from those who do not write. Writers are always absorbing ideas that they might distill into their writing some day.

Residents of Greenup County held Jesse Stuart in esteem but were also a little afraid of him. They never knew when *they* might become subjects for one of his pieces. Students understand. Their family members have been reluctant to be recorded on video while at a reunion or on vacation. Jesse wrote the truth. He saw people as they really were—not necessarily as they saw *themselves*. Even if the real names were disguised, Greenup was such a small place that everyone would know the person on whom Jesse's character was based.

Jessica's uncle used Jesse Stuart's works in his classes, and Jesse was kind enough to let him have several handwritten manuscripts. Jessica remembers Jesse Stuart's handwriting. She described it as very distinctive. Once you saw it, you would not forget it—many lower case letters, large cursive script. She compared his handwriting to a doctor's handwriting with lots of hurried scribbles. My students understand that Mr. Stuart was likely in a hurry to get his ideas on paper. They learn that every true writer cannot wait to get his or her ideas recorded. Jessica's uncle treasured the books Jesse gave him. They all had personal inscriptions. Jessica Adams loves Jesse Stuart's writing and looks forward to passing these books down to her own children some day.

From Jessica's family story, my students learn that Jesse Stuart loved his life in his east Kentucky hollow and that his love for *his people*—his Kentucky neighbors and friends—informed his writing. If Jesse Stuart were alive and teaching today, he would be first to say that forming a community of writers who read model Kentucky authors and who listen to classmates read their own stories with pride should be given first priority in the writing classroom.

CHAPTER SIXTEEN

At a joint meeting between several University of Kentucky colleges and the UK Community College system at the Carnahan House in Lexington, I had the opportunity to speak with professors who taught in the university's graduate and professional programs. I will never forget one conversation in particular because it began with a compliment from a medical school professor who had worked with one of my former students, Edith Rowe. Edith came to college when her children were college age themselves. With her children raised, her life was settling down, and she was ready to return to school to pursue dreams that had been put on hold for the sake of her family. The medical school professor recalled Edith's abilities, preparation, and ambition. She had transferred to the University of Kentucky to obtain her degree as a PA (physician's assistant). She is now a physician's assistant practicing at the Veterans' Hospital in Huntington, West Virginia.

I remember Edith as the student who reinforced the way I grade. I could not have taught writing thirty years without discovering an effective way to assign grades. My correcting technique began in northern Kentucky when a student told me about an incident that had occurred in another English teacher's class.

Everyone knows that secondary teachers are overworked. In the mid seventies that statement was as true as it is today, for high school teachers had no planning periods or breaks, and lunch times were duty periods. In addition to maintaining classroom discipline, teachers were required to monitor students' behavior in the hallways, in the cafeteria, and in the restrooms. When any student misbehaved, the first question asked of that student was, "Who is your teacher?" If a teacher dared to enjoy a bite of food without maintaining his or her peripheral focus on students, that teacher would be in trouble. The principal considered his primary job to be monitoring the *teachers*—not the *students*, reasoning that there were fewer teachers than students, and that they depended upon him for their annual evaluations. First to suffer in a stress-filled situation such as this is quality of instruction. Second is time spent actually *teaching*. Last, teachers simply do not have the time to grade assignments thoroughly.

A story told to me by my northern Kentucky student changed the way I grade papers today. He said that he had long suspected that one teacher did not read his work, but instead made a general comment on page one that could be made for any student and gave him a grade similar to grades he had received all year. To test his theory, he randomly repeated the words "peanut butter" throughout his composition. Sure enough, the paper was returned to him with the same grade he always received and with no mention of the unusual addition.

I thought about my own grading of compositions and was sure that such a sneaky trick could have been played on me in the past because once I felt I knew a student, I expected the same quality of work from that student time after time. Pressed for time and with hundreds of essays to grade, I had probably done quite a bit of skimming and skipping myself while reading students' papers. That day I began to mark compositions and journals differently. I decided to make comments in the margins in order to prove to students that

I had read closely. I began writing comments such as: "I understand," "I laughed out loud when I read this part," "I can relate," "Sad," etc. I knew that these comments were far more important than corrections about punctuation, pronoun reference, or subject-verb agreement. Students will only accept corrections and suggestions for improvement if they are convinced that their instructor has closely read the content. Even mechanics corrections can include a check mark and comments such as "correctly punctuated," "excellent transition," or "Yes, the comma belongs inside the closing set of quotation marks."

This method of marking compositions was reinforced by the experience I had with Edith. Edith surprised me one day after class with a comment. She had handed in her journal for me to grade. My journal grading system was based on positive reinforcement and correction/teaching of writing mechanics. I marked entries with a +2 or a +4 indicating the number of bonus points the entries deserved for the quality of writing. When students made several errors and obviously needed help with their writing skills, I would assign no bonus points. I would simply mark corrections and provide suggestions for improvements, but where I saw evidence of excellent, competent writing I would write a compliment and include an explanation that these were bonus points toward the final grade. By not taking points away and instead encouraging effective writing with a reward, I hoped to encourage students to try to develop their voices.

Edith said she had never been rewarded with a positive comment about her writing. She had assumed that college teachers used the same shade of red that high school teachers used to mark errors. On one of her journal entries, I had written a reaction. I remembered from the "peanut butter" incident that students wanted to know that their words had been thoughtfully read. Students care more about the quality of their writing if they know it is being read by a careful reader.

Through a lifetime of reading, Edith had matured into a talented writer, capable of letting the reader experience the events narrated along with her. She lacked self-confidence though, and assumed that each nineteen-year-old student in class was a better-prepared writer than she. I remember being pleased as Edith gained self-confidence about her writing. As she listened to other students read their papers for peer review, she could take pride in the fact that she had something to say that others wanted to hear. One of her papers was extremely memorable. In it she included the interview she did with a legend in our community, Doctor Paul B. Hall.

Doctor Hall is one of those people who stays in a place and makes a difference but one whose fame goes no farther. Just months before the interview his wife had passed. Doctor Hall was in a reflective mood as he responded to Edith's comments and questions: "You sure seem to enjoy life."

"Oh, I did up until six months ago when my wife died. See that picture up there. That's her."

"She was a beautiful woman. Was it easy or difficult raising your family in a rural east Kentucky community?"

"Oh, my wife took care of all that (raising the children). She was a wonderful mother."

Doctor Hall's humility waned as he began to speak about his medical training at the University of Kentucky and later at the University of Louisville. He was also proud that he had been recruited as a professional baseball player. He described athletics at UK during a time when basketball was an intramural afterthought; baseball was king. He teased his interviewer with a question about the state-of-the-art medical center in Paintsville that bears his name today: "Now what's the name of the new medical center?"

"I believe that might be Paul B. Hall Regional Medical Center."

Although he had a lifetime of achievements in the medical field, Doctor Hall recalled most poignantly a time of failure in his medical career. It was during the great influenza epidemic of the early 1900's: "I went to Louisville to train in the treatment of this disease that was killing so many of my neighbors. They taught us as much as possible and sent us home to do what we could to help the suffering. I remember up hollows in Van Lear (an east Kentucky coal camp) visiting one home where six family members lay dying."

As my class listened to the taped interview and later heard Edith's paper incorporating it, they were listening to the voice of a legend in our community but also to a man who was only human, experienced successes and failures during his career. Like all of us he simply did the best he could.

Doctor Paul B. Hall grew up in Concord, Kentucky, alongside the Big Sandy River where he knew and recognized the sounds of steam whistles from the packet steamboats that navigated the Big Sandy. They navigated as far upstream as Paintsville, bringing supplies such as sugar and salt that could not be produced in the region. One of his cousins played calliope on the John Davis boat. Doctor Hall attended a one-room school for the first eight years and then attended Paintsville High School where he received excellent preparation for his college classes that would earn him his medical degree.

During Doctor Hall's early medical practice he rode horseback to the homes of his patients. He recalled with joy delivering babies in his home county of Johnson as well as in the surrounding counties of Magoffin, Lawrence, and Martin. He remembered delivering as many as thirty-two babies in one month. These horseback rides were in all types of weather conditions, and, as most of the country roads in the mountains at the time were beside and in and out of creek beds, his feet would become wet from the splashing water and literally *freeze* to the stirrups. Upon his return home, his wife would meet him with a pan of hot water in order to thaw his feet from the stirrups so that he could dismount.

He owned the first automobile in Paintsville, a Dodge, but his favorite make of automobile, Buick, eventually replaced that old Dodge and several horses as his favorite means of transportation. As evidence of community support for his medical practice, he recalled fondly that the owner of the local Buick dealership would trade for his old car every year when the new models arrived. "I would give him my old car and a one hundred dollar bill, and he would give me a new Buick so that I could continue to have dependable transportation for my practice."

Throughout the first eighty years of the twentieth century Doctor Hall's experience had been one of neighbor helping neighbor: "Almost every young Johnson Countian who wanted to become a doctor has sat in this living room here, telling me about wanting to become a doctor and asking my advice. Without exception they all wanted my recommendation to medical school, and in exchange, they all promised to return to the mountains to practice and help the people here. But then they would go off to medical school, meet someone whom they wanted to marry and forget their promise."

Unkept promises did not keep Doctor Hall from offering his help to those who asked for it. Schools routinely made calls to check up on candidates to be considered for admission into their programs. Professors would call the local post office and inquire about a boy or girl's character and family support. One call would invariably be made to Doctor Hall to ask him for recommendation.

Doctor Hall's answers to Edith's interview questions at times came haltingly. There would be a long pause. Then Edith would repeat the question. Then another pause would follow before Doctor Hall finally got around to answering. We wondered about his health and age and thought him tired, but Edith was quick to correct our thinking by explaining that he was watching a golf match on TV at the time of the interview and was often distracted by his interest in the game. Anyone who knew Doctor Hall understood his love for the game of golf. He sat on the board of directors for the Paintsville course that sits on land that once belonged to his wife's family. He took pride in showing off the first eighteen-hole course in the mountains to visitors from other parts of the state. One such frequent visitor was former governor and National Baseball League commissioner, A. B. Happy Chandler. Doctor Hall became excited when he spoke of his friendship with Mr. Chandler. Some of the older students in class and I recalled Mr. Chandler's singing of *My Old Kentucky Home* at UK basketball games and his often quoted statement, "I never saw a Kentuckian who wasn't going home, if not at that moment in time, at some near point in the future." That quote says so much about his love and attachment for the state of Kentucky—sentiment shared by Dr. Hall for the state as well as for his home county. Their friendship was based on more than the game of golf.

Doctor Hall's fame may not have spread as widely as Governor Chandler's, but he made a difference in his place and touched the heart of a student of mine as she incorporated his words into a wonderful interview-based research paper about the practice of medicine in east Kentucky. I am proud that she successfully completed the physician's assistant program at the University of Kentucky, and from the professor who took the time to speak to me about her, I know she carried confidence into her course work there and that her teachers were as proud of her as I.

A friend and colleague of Doctor Hall's was Doctor John Turner whose stories about mountain people, including one legendary female country music performer, taught my students that success can result from humble beginnings.

Doctor John Turner was interviewed for my class. He, like Dr. Hall, practiced medicine in the mountains during the days when doctors made house calls. In fact he owned two Jeeps for this purpose. Like Dr. Hall he completed his medical training at the University of Louisville Medical School. One of his first medical positions was with Consolidated Coal Corporation where he was the coal camp doctor for the community of Jenkins. Later he held the same position in Van Lear, Kentucky, birthplace of Loretta Lynn. He was her doctor when she was a little girl, coming by his office after school to ask for cough medicine. He remembered that she would hold out her arm to volunteer to be first to take a vaccination. He told her she was pregnant with her first child when she did not understand why she had missed her monthly cycle. He delivered two of her babies and has maintained a close personal friendship with her over the years. She stays in his Big Sandy River Valley home when she is in the mountains performing a concert. In his new home there is even a Loretta Lynn bedroom painted in her favorite color.

Loretta Lynn was born eight miles from Big Sandy Community and Technical College in Butcher Hollow near the former coal camp town of Van Lear, Kentucky, where my mother was also born. Visitors to her home place come from all over the world. A Kentucky Department of Highways road sign points the way from Highway 321 (formerly Route 23) connecting Paintsville to Prestonsburg. If you go, be sure to stop by Words 'N Stuff bookstore in Powell addition before you make the final turn toward Van Lear and the hollow she made famous. Jim Trammel will be happy to tell you stories about the entertainer and her family as well as provide you with a map and directions to her home. Jim and wife Ann attend the Kentucky Book Fair in Frankfort each fall scouting out new Kentucky writers and have the most complete selection of books by Kentucky writers in the Big Sandy Valley. Jim and Ann meet thousands of people each summer as tourists in automobiles and on tour busses stop in to make sure they are on the correct path to Loretta Lynn's home.

After leaving the bookstore you are soon in the town of Van Lear where you may want to stop at an historical museum maintained by the Van Lear Historical Society. Inside is a scale model of the town when it was a working coal camp, mining memorabilia, and the restored office of Loretta Lynn's family doctor, Dr. John Turner.

My mother was born in Van Lear where my grandfather Millard Huff worked until the mines shut down, forcing him to move to Holden, West Virginia, to continue mining coal. My mother remembered the rumble of coal trains she heard when she was a little girl. CSX coal trains still roll on those same tracks alongside the Big Sandy River, carrying coal from east Kentucky preparation plants to the AEP power plant near Louisa or to barge loading facilities near the mouth of the Big Sandy. When I hear them or their warning whistles as they approach crossings, I picture my mother hiding underneath the kitchen table afraid of them. The tracks burdened from the weight of coal cars screeched like nails on a chalkboard. They were so close that the dishes rattled in the pie safe as they passed.

I was teaching in northern Kentucky when the book *Coal Miner's*

Daughter was published. I read it eagerly since it was written about my home. I watched the movie on the day of its release, and although most of the movie was filmed in Letcher County, to me the hills looked just like the hills of Loretta's and my home—Johnson County. I recognized my own homesickness but at the time didn't realize that reading the book and seeing the movie would start me on the path back home.

Those who have seen the movie or read the book will recall the little red forties Willy's Jeep that was the first "car" in which Loretta rode. The first symptom of my homesickness was my drive to Louisville where I traded in the first new car I had ever owned, a beautiful 1976 Pontiac Grand Prix, for a soft-top Jeep CJ7 Wrangler. My wife and I wound up driving this Jeep down "death hill" on I-75 into Cincinnati to graduate school. Since the Jeep had no air conditioner, those summers we drove each day to Xavier University's campus for graduate classes are memorable ones to say the least. On the way home to the mountains though, that Jeep was pure Heaven! I would turn off the Mountain Parkway at the Slade/Natural Bridge exit, stop to take the top down so that we could take what we called in those days " Jeep drives." Slowly we would drive along the hemlock shaded two-lane road leading into Daniel Boone National Forest and the Red River Gorge Area. The aroma of hemlocks, white pines, and wild roses as well as the sounds of mountain streams took me back home. I don't think my wife would agree that the Jeep trade was such a good one, but to me it was worth every minute spent in Cincinnati traffic. *Coal Miner's Daughter* began a cycle of events that would eventually lead me home.

Loretta Lynn's brother, Herman Webb, lives near the home place where he operates a country store filled with treasures from Loretta and sister Crystal Gayle's home. KET produced a wonderful episode of *Kentucky Life*, which featured host Dave Shuffett interviewing Mr. Webb. The interview perfectly captures Herman Webb's personality. Mr. Webb is a humble, quiet, kind man who is as proud of his family's past as he is of his sister's international fame. He recalls experiences similar to my own growing up in rural Johnson County. He played in the hills with a freedom not found in the play of city children in Paintsville. After several years spent in Indiana working in factories, he returned to east Kentucky where, he says, "I don't owe anybody anything."

The old home where they grew up is not far from the general store, near the head of Butcher Hollow. Mr. Webb will be glad to go with visitors to give them a personal tour of the home place. Visitors will be surprised to see that the old house is not really a cabin at all. The rooms are small. There is an old cast-iron hearth surrounding the fireplace. A traditional long porch fronts the house. The porch sits up high enough for children to play under, as Herman and Loretta must have done. The way they lived was not so different from the way any family in the mountains lived at the time. Her father mined coal and farmed, so that placed him in the same financial circumstances as my grandfather. My mother never remembered feeling poor when she was growing up, and I suppose Loretta Lynn felt likewise until she left east Kentucky and saw that in cities across the country lived another class of people.

Herman Webb performed in a country band on weekends and time off from work. He never quit his day job for the sake of a career in country music. He did, however, leave his factory job behind to return home to the mountains.

Students who become acquainted with Mr. Webb learn as much about the simple way of life he has chosen as they do about the life of his famous sister. Loretta Lynn's music career and books have put Butcher Hollow on the international map. A community whose economy depends on a single industry, the coal industry, needs the dollars tourism brings, but I wonder whether visitors to Loretta Lynn's Butcher Hollow home spend the time to see the fog as it lifts from the mountain valley after a rain or listen to the morning song-birds. I wonder if they discover the reason Herman Webb came back home.

Upward mobility in the mountains is not unusual, but it is normally accomplished in small steps rather than the leap Loretta Lynn's talent allowed her to make. In families where the parents have eighth-grade educations, children usually set goals just high enough to reach, but few set these goals so lofty as becoming a doctor. Edith Rowe's last interview question of Dr. Paul B. Hall was this: "Do you think that raising your children in the mountains was more difficult than it would have been in a larger city like Lexington or Louisville, and do you think that living here places limits on children?" I will never forget his reply: "Shucks, you can go to school and get the same education here that you can anywhere else. It's all up to the *individual*."

Chapter Seventeen

Another doctor who visited my classroom did so by way of his *writing* as well as the story of his mountain medical practice, for he was a doctor *and* a writer. His name was Doctor Francis Elam Burgess. After graduating from the University of Kentucky, Doctor Burgess attended the University of Louisville School of Medicine. He interned in Akron, Ohio and studied post-graduate surgery at Cook County Hospital, Chicago, Illinois. In 1939, he began private practice in Martin, Kentucky and also served on the staff of Prestonsburg General Hospital, Riverview Hospital in Louisa, as well as Paintsville Clinic.

I learned of Doctor Burgess from a Martin County student of mine Amanda Guyton, who, for her first assignment in my writing class, wrote a descriptive paper about him and his home. Actually, the paper became a narrative filled with description as my student told the story of her family's first encounter with the mountain doctor. Amanda's mother Mrs. Jeanette Guyton was a home health care nurse traveling to work in Louisa when her car broke down alongside Route 23 in the community of Kise, just north of Lowmansville in Lawrence County. She walked to the only nearby home, a gray fieldstone farm home on the Big Sandy River-bottom side of the highway. Once on the porch of the house, she discovered the front door slightly ajar. She knocked, and from inside stepped a tall but stooped gentleman with long white hair. His clothes were wrinkled as if they had been slept in, and he appeared to be malnourished. Mrs. Guyton discovered that Doctor Burgess was living there alone.

Mrs. Guyton was concerned about the health of Doctor Burgess and so began to stop in to check on him each day on her way to work, always bringing him something she had prepared to eat. He said he had no relatives living close by. He told her stories of visitors who had entered his home only to steal from him. He was becoming more and more afraid there living alone. His family's bottomland farm that stretched out for acres and acres had once sustained but now isolated him. He never married. Instead his older brother and he had continued to work the farm until his brother's death.

Since he could no longer live alone, my student's mother took Doctor Burgess into her home. He developed Alzheimer's disease. Mrs. Guyton and her family cared for him until he died. Amanda, my student, shared the story of Doctor Burgess, not because she or her family wanted recognition for their acts of kindness toward a stranger, but because she had come to think of him as a member of her family, one who was blessed with a special gift for writing poetry.

Confirmation of the story came from another student of mine who knew both Doctor Burgess and the family who took him in. Samantha Mills first recalled meeting Doctor Burgess when she was a little girl. Her father had done some work for him on the farm, and she had tagged along. She told me that he was always reciting poems for people. He would go up to complete strangers in shopping center parking lots and recite poems for them. In Samantha's case the poem he recited was about an opossum. Its title was "A Slick Tail 'Possum." He had given her a copy of his collection of poems, *Echoes From the Highlands,* in which the poem was included. She had treasured it through the years, and even so, agreed to let me borrow it.

As I read, I discovered beautiful personal poetry about his early medical career, his relationships, friends, and acquaintances. One poem was written and likely recited for the clerks who worked at the nearby convenience store. The closest place of business—the *only* store nearby his farm—was a Happy Mart. He called the poem "My Happy Mart Helpers." I could feel the relief from loneliness he experienced upon talking with store clerks, possibly the only living souls he had seen or spoken to in weeks.

Another poem, "These Are Not the Good Old Days," tells the story of a stranger who knocked on his door and gained entry to use the phone, only to steal his watch. Doc's first thought was never to trust a stranger again, but then he reminded himself that only Jesus did not sin, and he closed the poem with a prayer that the thief would find God some day. Two of his poems, "A Doctor's

Dr. Burgess Home on Route 23, Kise, KY.

Reflection" and "A Tribute To My Father" were written about his father whom he describes as a poor farmer who never allowed a traveler who stopped by his home for a drink of water to go without being fed as well. His father had instructed him when he became a doctor to "make your charge easy on the poor."

In another poem I learned that he was a flight surgeon in World War II serving aboard the destroyer U.S.S. Lindsey during the U.S. invasion of Iwo Jima and Okinawa. He was wounded when his ship was cut in two by a pair of Japanese Kamikaze bombers and was awarded the Purple Heart. Other poems were written upon the loss of his brother and sisters. In one poem he wrote about opening the barns to care for animals in winter, and in another about the guilt he felt after having once killed a deer. In still another poem titled "A House of Stone" he described his home, which was constructed in 1850 and is included in the National Registry of Historic Places. Regarding the permanence of his home he stated, " 'Till the end of time it'll be there still."

I discovered through reading Dr. Burgess' poems that he was an admirer and close observer of nature, a romantic, who had exchanged his medical practice, (He retired from medical practice in 1951) for a life of farming and writing. When I read my poems for the public today, I often read a poem I wrote in tribute to the mountain doctor/writer titled "For Doctor Burgess." Listeners will sometimes say to me after the reading that they once met this genuine, compassionate man. Some even say he recited a poem for them. Today as I drive by the deserted stone house on my way to Ashland or to Huntington, I think of him and hope his last days were filled with the same happiness he gave children and adults to whom he once recited his poems.

We drove by your house today.
You were not at home,
Haven't been for years now.
The gray stone farmhouse was falling into disrepair
As all vacant houses do.

Your Big Sandy River bottom home place
Drew our notice long before we heard your story.
Now that one you touched
Has come my way—a student in my class—
I imagine you seated there on front porch swing, pen in hand.

I always knew this spruce shrouded home
Between Lowmansville and Louisa
Was the home of a poet—
Something about the way it was set in the river valley—
Open to water and the sky.

When I mention your old home to my students now
In the effort to share still another local author,
Almost all have noticed your place on their way to the malls.
Some have wondered as I once did
About the life once lived there.

Softer hearts have even noticed
The yellow tape encircling the porch,
Proclaiming the house condemned.
The thought of no one allowed to enter
Saddens them.

One student's eyes brightened
When I read your poem about your career as a mountain doctor.

She remembered meeting you when she was a little girl.
You read a poem for her about a 'possum.
She had kept the copy you gave her all these years.

You also gave her your book of poems.
She shared them with me—let me keep them together longer than I should.
Somehow she understood
I needed to know you better.
She said your door had always been open to strangers.

She shared more than your writing with me,
Told me of your way with children though you were not a father,
Told of your never having sold a poem.
You always gave poems away
As they had been given to you.

She said you enjoyed reciting.
The convenience store clerk,
Who worked in a store near your farm,
Said you often
Gave her poems this way.

Each time we drive by your home place now
I mention your name to my family.
Sixteen years ago you introduced poetry to a shy little girl.
She has passed on your words to others as you knew she would.
Eyes closed, we see you in that porch swing writing still.

CHAPTER EIGHTEEN

Mountain students share not only a common heritage but also a history of belonging to a close community of family and friends who enjoyed being *entertained*. The mountain storytelling tradition once unified generations within families and was handed down before the wide availability of books and prior to the early beginnings of other entertainment venues. Radio and movies were first to begin to take the place of storytelling, but radio was most like storytelling because it continued to allow listeners to use their imaginations.

For me the next best thing to reading was, as I was growing up and to this day, listening to the radio where the storytelling tradition lives on through words and songs. My hometown of Paintsville, as was the case with most rural towns in the fifties and sixties, had but one radio station. Mine was the AM-band era, and although my choice of stations was principally limited to Paintsville's WSIP and WDOC in Prestonsburg (which came in with static), nightfall brought the world to my east Kentucky pillow. My father bought my brother and me a single Murphy's five-and-ten store guitar to share one Christmas, but when we asked for the newest invention in radio—transistor radios, he knew our sharing one would be out of the question. Besides, Daddy knew Clyde Music who worked in the local hardware store where transistor radios were sold. He had "made Clyde a good price" on a set of tires recently and felt comfortable and proud to be able to haggle him down on the cost of two Panasonic nine-transistor radios. Mine was black and chrome with a vertical dial along one edge with a wrist strap that was not needed because the radio fit in the palm of one hand. It even came with an ivory ear phone which I seldom found use for because I preferred holding the radio's speaker up to my ear or placing it beneath my pillow at night when my parents thought I was asleep.

At night faraway stations came in crystal clear. I listened to stations like WWL in New Orleans, Louisiana, WOWO in Fort Wayne, Indiana, WSM in Nashville, Tennessee, WRVA in Richmond, Virginia, and WLW in Cincinnati, Ohio. I enjoyed local radio in the daytime because Paintsville radio's Bill Barker came into our homes—an invited guest—as if he were a friend of the family. But at night when I could listen to distant AM stations, I had the opportunity to travel to places I'd never been and thought I might never see.

Young people today do not really *get* radio. They listen for the music when they do not have access to CDs or MP 3s. Today when I ask my students if they listen to National Public Radio, (Two NPR stations are available in the mountains: WEKU in Richmond and WMSU in Morehead), the response is not only a negative one, but most do not even realize what National Public Radio *is*. If, while scanning the dial, they have heard our two public radio stations at all, they have quickly dismissed them as classical music stations and just as quickly switched to another station. I introduce my students to some of Public Radio International's content by going on line to record Garrison Keillor's wonderful daily five-minute segment on writing called *The Writers' Almanac* at www.writersalmanac.publicradio.org. He gives a brief biography of famous writers born on each date and concludes by reading a poem. I am hopeful that once students hear and enjoy the program, they might take the time to listen to public radio themselves.

When I bring recorded radio programs into my college classroom today, I enjoy noticing the expressions on my students' faces as they focus on what they are hearing. At first they have trouble focusing their attention on the broadcast. It is almost like introducing a toddler to its first book. Getting the child to sit still and pay close attention is the first step in promoting a lifetime love for reading. As they listen to radio, students must learn to concentrate and use their imaginations, the same skills they learned when their parents read books to them. (Hopefully their parents *did* read to them.) Watching TV and movies or playing video games does not allow for use of the imagination. On-air essays and stories, both feature and news stories, provide listeners the same framework that books provide readers. Readers and listeners fill in the spaces by using their own imaginations.

When my children were small, I would play a trick on them by taking them with me on a boat we kept docked at Paintsville Lake Marina. Once we were out on the lake together, they were *trapped*. Not only were we together as a family in a small space where it was impossible for them to go to separate rooms, but we also were in a peaceful place to read together or to listen to the radio. I always kept a book or two on the boat, and a battery operated radio on which National Public Radio came in clearly. They grew up listening to Bob Edwards interviews and guest essays on "Morning Edition" or Michael Feldman talking with writers like Grundy, Virginia, native, Lee Smith, or Brooksville, Kentucky, native, Ed McClanahan, on his weekly show "What Do You Know?"

My son and daughter became good listeners and readers because they developed a love for both. When ex-English teacher himself,

Michael Feldman, brought the live broadcast of his "What Do You Know?" to the campus of my alma mater EKU, my family had the opportunity to watch production of live radio. My son recently graduated from Northern Kentucky University's College of Professional Studies with a major in radio/TV communication. He had the opportunity to intern on WNKU, Northern's National Public Radio affiliate where his familiarity with public radio provided a foundation for further learning.

The real reason young people should be exposed to public radio just as they should be exposed to books is not to inspire them to become broadcasters or writers. The ability they develop to concentrate and use their imaginations while reading or listening will help them throughout their educations and will enhance their enjoyment of life. Today my children understand what I was doing on those mornings when I took them with me on the boat. I hope they have their own boats some day or a least a comfortable couch in a room with *only* books and radio—no TV.

A single TV station, WYMT, in Hazard, serves the east Kentucky mountains. The station has a Big Sandy Bureau and does a good job of covering news in the valley. Still, the towns of Paintsville, Pikeville, Prestonsburg, Inez, and Salyersville, the county seats in the Big Sandy Community and Technical College service area, have no television station of their own. That void has been filled by a long list of radio stations up and down the Big Sandy Valley.

Radio in the mountains has provided an invaluable service. Local newsgathering and reporting have been priorities as has been live coverage of local sports. In fact, several radio sportscasters from the mountains have become legends. Harlan County's Caywood Ledford became a *statewide* legend as broadcaster of the University of Kentucky Wildcats for nearly four decades as well as national broadcaster of the Kentucky Derby for CBS. A retirement jersey hangs in his honor from the rafters of Rupp Arena. Jim Fyffe, a Johnson County native, who began his radio career broadcasting the Johnson Central Golden Eagles and the Paintsville Tigers on WSIP, was for more than twenty years radio voice of the Auburn University Tigers. Doug Ormay, who today broadcasts the University of Louisville basketball games as well as other news and sports on the Kentucky News Network, also began his broadcasting career in Paintsville. He gained a statewide audience while broadcasting the Kentucky State Boys Sweet Sixteen Basketball Tournament.

People in the mountains take their radio seriously. Radio in the mountains is a reflection of the culture. On-air traditions have survived changes in contemporary society. One of these traditions is the reading of obituaries. People from larger cities who have moved to the mountains are unaccustomed to hearing obituaries read on radio. The reading of obituaries is still *the* most serious and important part of an east Kentucky DJ's job. Reading an obituary is the last opportunity the community has to honor the lives of our people who have passed. Mountain people "know when you are sick and care when you die."

As a boy I don't recall many places of business in Paintsville where one could not hear WSIP in the background, as men like my father did their day's work. On-air personalities were *friends*— literally. Dad knew Bill Barker, morning radio personality on WSIP. Mr. Barker joined the staff of the first Paintsville radio station upon its opening in 1949. He was an institution in east Kentucky radio for more than thirty-five years. When I visited the studio for the first time with my third-grade classmates to read poems we had written, I remember the *thrill* I felt when Mr. Barker patted the top of my head and asked me about my daddy. I thought I must be someone very special if a man as important as Bill Barker knew my father.

Each morning as my mother prepared breakfast, the singing of Patsy Cline or George Jones could be heard coming from a portable Motorola radio. Between songs as we would be finishing our eggs and gravy, Bill Barker would slurp his coffee and *talk* to us. He would tell a joke or a story about meeting one of the country music artists. Then he would do his own commercials, again *talking* to us about businesses and services that had paid for airtime. Bill Barker was a part of our community. Everybody knew him, whose boy he was, where he lived, and where he was from—Waller Hole in Elliott County. Most knew he had been in a country band, The Brown Mountain Boys, performing through northern states for homesick east Kentuckians. He played bass fiddle and sang.

When Bill Barker advertised a business in town, we *believed* what he said. We knew he bought groceries from Home Cash Grocery on Court Street or from Cousin Clyde's on old Route 40 west. Sometimes he would call Cousin Clyde himself and allow him to advertise weekly specials. Ellis Hamilton would call in to describe the properties his real estate company had recently acquired.

Those who were not born and raised in the east Kentucky mountains do not understand the popularity of live remotes from businesses for advertising. They marvel at owners of local businesses like Malcolm Ratliff, owner of B and W TV and Appliance, who pay for time to call in and go on air to advertise their products and prices. By the way the W in B and W TV and Appliance stands for Williams, the name of one of the prior owners. Everett Williams made the business so successful that Malcolm would not dare change the name today. Mr. Williams' success was due to the same live call-in commercials that Malcom uses today.

Nolan Hall, another radio personality in the mountains, has disk jockeyed at stations in Prestonsburg, Pikeville, Martin, Salyersville, and Williamson, West Virginia. He was on the air at WXCC, Coal Country Radio 96.5, when a Martin County student of mine heard him speak at a Charleston, West Virginia, political rally in support of coal industry issues. The Pike County native explained in the interview he did for one of my students that his major influence while growing up in the mountains was listening to Bill Barker. If it weren't for Bill Barker, he would never have been in radio. While Nolan "Country Cousin" Hall was DJ at the Salyersville radio station, he called Bill Barker at home each morning to allow listeners to once again hear his voice and his famous slurping of coffee.

Radio stations today are losing the community of listeners they once attracted by distancing themselves from the people they originally were intended to serve. Personalities of the DJs have become subordinate to computer-driven play lists, satellite feeds and downloads, and over-produced, media-company-created commercials.

Nolan Hall considers himself a throwback to the past of mountain radio. He takes pride in the ability to communicate with his audience and entertain them while always being himself and telling them the truth. I remember once when he had been involved in a serious accident, his Magoffin County fans were so concerned about him that the station owner, local attorney C. K. Belhasen, called him and put him on air from his hospital bed so that fans would hear his voice, know that he was recovering, and understand that he would soon be on the air again.

Mr. Hall explained the approach he takes to his profession. He said, "When I am talking on air, Susan, I am speaking directly to *you*. I try to imagine that I am speaking to a single person. That person is not necessarily male or female—young or old—just someone who shares my interest in country and bluegrass music." I remembered how I had felt when Bill Barker was on air. That was it—the *secret*! Both Bill Barker and Nolan Hall were talking only to *me*. That's the way both made me feel as I listened.

When asked about the entertainers he had met over the past thirty-four years in the business, he mentioned Waylon Jennings, George Jones, Conway Twitty, Earnest Tubb, etc., but he took a special interest in relating the story of his first meeting with Keith Whitley. He described Keith as a close friend—not close in the sense that one might brag about knowing a star—but sincerely close. Handshakes were not enough between the two. Keith always hugged his neck and treated him like a brother. Mr. Hall said that Keith Whitley was a genuine man *first* and an entertainer second. He had the mountain quality of humility which made his fans appreciate *him* as much as his music.

As we finished listening to the interview with Nolan Hall, I noticed a hand raised and waving in the air. A student who came to the mountains from Jacksonville, Florida, couldn't wait to explain to her fellow students, natives of east Kentucky, that radio here was one of the first cultural differences she had noticed. She mentioned her shock at hearing obituaries read on air as well as her surprise upon hearing informal advertisements delivered by business owners. Now she understood.

Newcomers to the mountains need to understand and appreciate the cultural differences they find upon their arrival. But even more important is the need for mountain students to realize that their differences come from a proud history and a close community of family and friends.

CHAPTER NINETEEN

During the sixties and seventies, one airport served our part of the Big Sandy Valley—the Bert T. Combs Airport located beside Route 23 midway between Paintsville and Prestonsburg. The airport was built on land still known as Blockhouse Bottom, the site of the first permanent settlement in Kentucky, Harmon Station. Harmon Station is the fort to which Jenny Wiley made her famous escape from her native captors.

The small airport made quite an impact on the community in the sixties, and although it is still home to a few private planes, the old Combs Airport has been virtually replaced by the new Regional Airport located near a newly constructed federal prison on land reclaimed from the surface-mining of coal. Large tracts of flat land are scarce in the mountains. The fact that the land occupied by the old airport has not been purchased for development of another kind is probably due to the location itself, which is in the flood plain of the Big Sandy River. Also Route 23 has moved across the river and mountains and now follows a more direct route between Paintsville and Prestonsburg.

The little Combs Airport never gained so much attention as it did in 1964, when President Lyndon B. Johnson's helicopter came to rest there. Although local politics have always been important in the mountains, east Kentucky has never been a hotbed for national politics. In fact, the closest a Presidential candidate had ever come to our area was once when John F. Kennedy visited Huntington, West Virginia during the 1959 Kennedy/Nixon campaign.

I did not shake President Johnson's hand, but I knew people who did, and I remember seeing the caravan of black Lincoln Continental limousines as it made its way down Third Street, turning onto Court Street and stopping in front of the Johnson County Court House. The Johnson County appearance did not make the national headlines as did the President's Martin County visit, for Martin County had the unwanted distinction of being one of the poorest counties in the nation and had been singled out for the public relations purpose of launching President Johnson's federal war on poverty.

The mother of one of my students recalled the visit and associated it with the fear she remembered feeling at the time. She remembered hearing her mother yell to her and her brothers and sisters from the front door of their modest home. Being called to come inside in the middle of a hot summer afternoon with no threat of storm was unusual, and she remembered fearing the worst. Her mother explained that she had just seen a news bulletin on TV while watching her "stories," the mountain term for soap operas. In the bulletin, WSAZ's Boz Johnson had reported that the President had stopped to visit a family she knew. The house was on Rock Castle Creek just ten miles from their home on Milo. Her mother was horrified that the President's war on poverty had begun with a random stop at a shack that depicted the nation's view of abject poverty. Her mother knew the clan. She felt they got exactly what they deserved. Their father "wouldn't work in a pie factory" as the local saying went. A burlap coffee sack hung as a door, several cars sat rusting in the yard, and garbage had been thrown over the embankment in front of the house. The yard itself was bare, baked earth. The father kept the yard scratched clear of any grass so that he would not have to cut it. They "didn't have a chamber pot or a window to throw it through."

The mother just knew that the family would play the part of the illiterate hillbilly to the hilt. They would welcome the national attention that they would never understand, attention that would for years to come color the image the rest of the world would see of the east Kentucky mountain people.

As I think back on the poverty *I* grew up in, it seems there were two kinds: clean, honest hard-working poverty and dirty, lying "wouldn't work in a pie factory" poverty. I knew that I was poor. Comparing my family's circumstances and the living conditions of others in my class, to residents of the city of Paintsville, and to others whose lives I watched on our black and white TV, I was poor, but my father always had a job, and I never remember being dirty. No matter the condition of our rented house when we would move in, Mom would make it spotless in short order. She loved to paint, and took artistic pride in her work. I even remember one run-down shack my father rented for us from Howard Dills. It stood on stilts to keep it above Tom's Creek's frequent floods. In one of its four rooms, there was a fireplace made of brick. The chimney was not safe, and we could never have a real fire there. No house we ever lived in had a working fireplace. Hence every apartment, duplex, and home I have ever lived in has had one. What I recall about that particular hearth were the individual bricks that Mom painted candy-cane red. She used my brother's paint-by-number-set paintbrush to trim in white the mortar between each brick. Even if the fireplace could not be used, she wanted it to be beautiful. Painting ceilings and walls that did not belong to her became ritual for my mother. The only place she lived that she never painted was the twelve-foot wide trailer she died in. When Dad moved her into that mobile home, I really believe she took a look around and gave up her effort to make houses into homes.

On hands and knees my mother would wax our linoleum floors, shiny enough that I could see myself reflected. I remember the delicious smell of Johnson's paste wax. If there were a food that tasted like that smell, I would devour it today. The most expensive appliance in our home was always the Electrolux vacuum cleaner. I never understood why that was the one appliance we made payments on. Now I know it was because Mom knew she could keep our home cleaner with this brand. The sound of a vacuum today is a comfort to me—reminding me of the pride my mother took in working to make our home spotless. Everyone knew Daddy worked, and so we fell into the honest, hard-working poverty category.

My Martin County student's mother realized that the family, whom President Johnson had stopped to single out, fell into the latter category of poverty. They would not work even if given the chance and soon proved this. After the President's visit the father was placed on a county works project only to be let go for showing up for work drunk on shaving lotion.

The President had declared a war on poverty but had prepared no strategy to win it. Handouts would never teach a lazy person the value of hard work. Dirt would not wash off without effort. In east Kentucky those who do try are too often judged along with those who do not. Before helping people, it is first necessary to get to know them. Getting to know east Kentuckians was not in President Johnson's plans. Perhaps if it had been, he would have come to know that there were two types of poverty in the mountains of east Kentucky. People can lift themselves out of the clean, honest hardworking kind of poverty. Rising from the opposite kind is impossible. Handouts benefit neither.

Government handout programs came and went in the mountains,

but the televised family never got the pot or the window. None of the children graduated from high school. When the mother died, the father remarried a much younger woman who bore him two more children. One died, and when the other came to school drugged on Darvon, Social Services contacted the police. When the body of the dead child was exhumed, the cause of death was discovered to be an overdose of the same pain medication. The child had been sacrificed for a small sum of an insurance policy. The national media has long forgotten about the Martin County family once made famous by a President's visit.

Seldom does one media event create such an impact on a particular region as did the late eighties "48 Hours" feature titled "Another America." Verna Mae Slone said when asked what motivated her to write, that her son once said she wrote when something made her *mad*. She said that he would tell her to calm down first before putting something on paper. She is not an angry woman by nature, but as she wrote *What My Heart Wants To Tell*, she must have recalled the anger she felt when she read or saw something that portrayed her people in a negative and degrading light. In her preface, she writes a letter to her grandchildren—her original target audience—explaining to them her reason for writing. She was tired of young people from the mountains going into the cities for work or into the armed services being forced to deny their heritage and claim to be from somewhere else. She specifically mentions "The Beverly Hillbillies." She did not like the fact that our people were being turned into caricatures for the entertainment of the national viewing audience.

Executives at CBS recently considered producing a new reality version of the show, "The Beverly Hillbillies." Printed articles about the upcoming show stirred quite a controversy not just in the mountains of east Kentucky but in other southern states as well. Planning for the show progressed to the point that CBS began paying for advertisements on east Kentucky radio stations in order to recruit a poor family who would be willing to live in a Beverly Hills mansion and have their daily lives televised in Ozzy Osborne-like fashion.

When the "48 Hours" segment featuring Muddy Gut in Floyd County first aired, the program itself was quite new, and CBS was attempting to validate the show and attract an audience by using Dan Rather, whose journalistic credentials were respected, to do both the introduction and closing segments. Broadcasters at the local CBS affiliate, WYMT (We're Your Mountain Television), in Hazard, Kentucky learned in advance that the program's focus was negative and that the east Kentucky poor had been stereotypically portrayed without dignity. Wayne Martin, station manager, even considered not allowing the program to be locally broadcast. Instead, the station decided to allow its airing but also produced its own rebuttal to immediately follow. Mr. Martin realized that the documentary would infuriate his station's audience base.

Tony Turner, trusted WYMT news anchor, introduced and later interrupted "Another America" in order to tell the audience to stay tuned for the rebuttal. Dan Rather's comments framed the program itself. Rather said in his opening remarks that the road to progress in the mountains was paved with good intentions but that there was still poverty to be found in the mountains like none anywhere else in the country. In his closing, he implied that all mountain residents would leave if given the opportunity. I thought of the homeless I had seen on the streets of Manhattan, sleeping under cardboard boxes placed over steaming sewer vents and of the Washington DC homeless I had seen sleeping on statues. I then thought of the hitchhiker I had picked up at a gas station just off the Paintsville

Dr. Henry A. Campbell, Jr., founding President of Prestonsburg Community College

exit of US 23. He was without a home but headed back to Pike County where his family lived who would take care of him until he could get back on his feet. I thought of the fact that in all the time I had lived and taught in the mountains, other than that transient, I had never seen or heard of a homeless person.

Poverty *does* exist in the east Kentucky mountains. I, of all people, should know since I came from the working poor. Drugs have brought to the region its share of crime and violence. Alcohol addiction has intensified problems such as child and spouse abuse within mountain families. Government handouts have fostered a new generation of people who expect not to have to work but instead to have their income *given* to them. But as Verna Mae Slone said, "Show me a place where there is no poverty, violence, and crime." "Another America's" portrayal was of a place where the part represents the whole. Those with chemical abuse problems and those who are too lazy to work were said to be representative. We in the mountains of east Kentucky who *try*, who value hard work and education, are tired of being judged by those around us who don't try.

Days after the airing of the broadcast, the founding president of our college, Dr. Henry A. Campbell, Jr., made his own feelings clear in a specially called meeting in the Pike Auditorium on our campus. Doc had one ear always tuned to politics in the mountains, and he sensed right away what this "48 Hours" feature would do to slow progress. Industries looking to expand would want nothing to do with such a place as was portrayed in the program. Producers of the feature had deliberately ignored the college and some of the highest ranked school systems in the state located within its five-county service area in order to give the image of a culture that had devalued education and done nothing to solve its own problems.

The CBS producers evidently thought that the fact that entertainers such as Floyd County's Dwight Yoakum who had left the mountains and made it in the outside world were anomalies. An interview with the entertainer framed the program. Although Dwight Yoakum said he admired the strength and determination of the mountain people, negative images were flashed on the screen as he spoke those positive words. His song, "Readin', Writin', and Route 23," could be heard in the background as viewers saw images of front-yard hog lots, rusted yard cars and dirty-faced children. Once while being interviewed he stopped to discipline his dog with a strong warning. The interviewer asked in fear if Mr. Yoakum was speaking to the dog or to him. *Of course* he was speaking to the dog, and why did the angry command for the dog to obey not get edited out of the piece? It was left in intentionally to show the temper of a mountain man and how such a temper is to be feared by strangers daring to evoke it.

The song title "Readin', Writin', and Route 23" comes from a statement residents of Ohio were known to have made concerning education or lack of same in the Kentucky mountains: Kentucky children were supposedly taught these three subjects with the last being the most important—the road north out of the mountains. I strongly suspect that no one connected with the program had ever listened to the song in its entirety, for the real point of the song's lyrics is that taking US 23 north was a *mistake* for so many mountain people, as indeed it was for my own father. The road north did *not* lead out of misery but instead: "They didn't know that that old highway/ Would lead them to a world of misery." The misery is in Ohio—away from the mountaineer's native culture and family— *not* in the hills of home.

I use the program in my classes to inspire the anger that motivated Verna Mae Slone and others inside our culture to write about our people. I also use the piece to illustrate the power of the visual image and the ability of television producers to portray preconceived beliefs as truths and present distorted parts as representative. Many students have never watched television with a critical eye before. They learn not to blindly trust that the media will be fair in its reporting. They learn not only the value of critical thinking but also the importance of reading a variety of sources before making up their minds on an issue. They learn never to allow a TV program to do their research and their thinking for them.

"Another America" closes with a reporter interviewing a Johnson family member on a hilltop family cemetery. The reporter lacked any understanding of family cemeteries in the mountains. He did not know the reason we bury our dead on hilltops and not in valleys. Our forefathers needed every inch of valley land for farming. Nor did he understand the obligation we in the mountains inherit from our parents and grandparents to visit and maintain these family cemeteries. When I was a little boy, I was taught to respect those hilltop graves with the reprimand to never step on a grave. I felt as if "48 Hours" had done just that by not making the effort or taking the time to understand our culture.

WYMT news anchor Tony Turner died On June 30, 2002, after injuries he suffered in a car crash on US Highway 421 in Whitley County on his way home from covering a news story. I remember during the three weeks following the accident and preceding his death, the overwhelming outpouring of sympathy and concern that came from all over the Big Sandy Valley and other southeastern Kentucky counties in the WYMT viewing area. Many of my colleagues had met or worked with Tony over the years, and even those who had not, respected his professionalism and his dedication to serve the people of the mountains of east Kentucky.

The panel Mr. Turner invited to be a part of the "48 Hours" rebuttal was made up primarily of local community leaders. One of the panel members was Jane Bagby, Assistant Director of the Appalachian Center at the University of Kentucky. She said that her office had frequent communications with the producers of "Another America" and that although she offered the show's producers example after example of progress in east Kentucky, they were not looking for positives; they were looking for anything that would portray the mountains in a negative light consistent with their own preconceived ideas.

When I finished watching CBS's program, I remember feeling the most concern for the young people in our region who would quickly dismiss the portrayal but keep in the back of their minds the thought that they might need to deny their heritage and be ashamed of their culture. Young people from the mountains who have not traveled extensively tend to negatively view their home area because they have nothing to compare it to. They are aware of problems in their home counties because they read and hear about them in the local media. They read 911 reports in local weekly newspapers, and they hear about abuse within friends' families. What they fail to recognize is that no place is free of problems.

Ms. Bagby, the UK administrator, said students from the mountains sometimes come to the university, ashamed to say the names of places they are from. She said if the university can get them enrolled in an Appalachian Studies class, the chips on their shoulders can easily be removed. Students from east Kentucky welcome the opportunity such a class presents for them to express *pride* in their culture and heritage.

Another guest on Tony Turner's panel, Nancy Collins, a Hazard attorney, reminded me through her own comments of the way my wife felt about moving to the mountains. Ms. Collins was originally from western Kentucky and had lived for several years in Lexington before moving her practice to Perry County. She said that she had *wanted* to move to the mountains. She actually *preferred* living in east Kentucky to living in Lexington or in her home county. My wife grew up in Owen County and loves living in the mountains. She teaches in the Johnson County school system, academically one of the highest ranked systems in the state. When we moved to the mountains in 1984, she taught in the same rural elementary school

Linda Scott DeRosier attended. My wife noticed the family atmosphere there that Ms. DeRosier depicted in her memoir *Creeker* as well as the small school's close connection to the community it served. Children were members of a community where they cared about one another. Jesse Stuart's "spirit of the one-room school" that he felt should still survive in modern classrooms was alive and well at Meade Memorial Elementary School.

I wonder whether the producers of "Another America" referenced the sixties study of Appalachian east Kentucky, *Yesterday's People* by Jack E. Weller. As I show the program to my students, I stop the tape to read an excerpt of what was written about our people in that book so that my students will see the similarities.

There is a section on education in Weller's book for example, as there is in "Another America." Weller states that there is little desire for education on the part of mountain children. He says that young people are only interested in moving away, and this includes young teachers. Weller says that the best and brightest in the mountains are bright enough to leave, thus creating a constant drain that diminishes education.

CBS selected *the* most run-down high school in the mountains, Wheelwright High School, to represent education in the mountains. No other schools were filmed. Students interviewed were taken advantage of—thinking that they had no choice but to participate and respond to their interviewers. They said that someone did not care—not the teachers but someone else in authority in the Floyd County School system. Evidence was all around them in the form of decaying, crumbling facilities. What was never told was that the money had already been allocated and the plans had already been drawn for a new state-of-the-art school—South Floyd High. Wheelwright High School teachers and their principal were interviewed, but no one mentioned, *Mantrip,* the award-winning literary/cultural magazine produced at the school by students under the supervision of one of the most outstanding English teachers in the country, Carol Stumbo.

According to Weller, young girls in the mountains married early in order to escape the terrible conditions at home only to find themselves in the same poverty and climate for abuse they had been attempting to escape. "Another America" likewise portrayed a culture in the mountains that tolerates spouse abuse. The producers of "Another America" even found an interviewee who stated that mountain men acted as if the law still existed that permitted them to "beat their wives into submission." Women tolerated abuse at the insistence of their mothers who told them, "I stood it all those years. You can do likewise."

Producers found one young couple who were planning marriage, promised them a wedding video, and set about filming the wedding. The bride-to-be was filmed and interviewed while she held a baby—implication being that this would be her lot soon. The camera focused on poverty within the storefront church. We in the mountains have respect for each other's place and manner of worship, and although we realize not all churches have stained glass windows, carpeting, or magnificent church organs, we respect the ways and beliefs of each other, knowing the spirit of the Lord surely visits rich and poor alike. Producers made sure the viewing audience saw the toy organ used to play the wedding march and the reception complete with grocery cake and gallon jugs of store-bought punch. The audience was told that the couple left the ceremony to honeymoon as was typical in the mountains in a run-down local motel. In *Yesterday's People* Weller states that the happy couple usually returns home to the young man's parents both to honeymoon and then to begin living together since most who marry in the mountains do not have jobs. At least the groom in "Another America" had a job working in the coal mines, but the implication was that the "five-dollars-an hour" the job paid would hardly provide a way out of poverty. The only wedding video the couple received in exchange for allowing themselves to be videoed was the same taped copy I show to my students.

The view of our people and place did not change much in the thirty-four years between *Yesterday's People* and "Another America." Or could it be that the book became the script for a documentary whose main point was that nothing has changed in the east Kentucky mountains?

Cemeteries in the mountains are beautiful spiritual places where Verna Mae Slone says she can kneel and feel close to those who have passed, cry if she needs to, and come away refreshed with the feeling that her loved ones are still with her. "Another America" closed with a visit to the Johnson Cemetery. The family members who regularly visited their people's graves were pictured as curiosities who were content to live and die in squalor, "yesterday's people" who chose to live in the past. Ironically, I talked with Verna Mae Slone about Weller's book while visiting her home in 1988 prior to the filming of "Another America." She owned the book, and recalled the anger she felt upon reading it. Her anger motivated her writing. I will never forget her words about her mountain culture: "We are not 'yesterday's people.' We just *love* yesterday and have not forgotten it."

Dan Rather closes "Another America" with words those of us in the mountains who watched the program will never forget. He explained that according to a "University of Kentucky study," the residents of east Kentucky could not afford the gas money to leave the mountains. We can. We don't want to.

CHAPTER TWENTY

I love sharing personal anecdotes as I teach. As I grow older, I worry whether I may repeat myself, but I am sure students forgive me if I do, for they realize that I teach more than one section of the same course. One true anecdote that I relate each semester helps my students better understand the importance of considering their audience as they write. Writing can become a solitary activity, and although we must write to please ourselves, the story of reading before *my* first audience helps students understand how consideration of audience can improve their writing.

Ken with staff and faculty in a Pike Building classroom.

My family members were my first audience, and by *family* I refer to immediate family only. I wrote initially for my children, Stephen and Beth. Before I realized that I needed to write, I recognized that they were growing up without knowing their grandparents or great grandparents. I knew that I had to do something to fill the void, and writing stories about my people was the only way to do so. Each Sunday morning I would get up early before my wife or children awoke. I would open a window or door to feel the fog damp of a mountain morning and listen to the calls of mourning doves, cardinals, and blue jays as they echoed down the hillsides and through the hollow behind my home. The first poem I wrote was about storytelling itself. I imagined that stories originated from under a "rock house" that I could see through the family room door. There were several such rock overhangs in my past. One was alongside a swimming hole on Hood's Creek where I used to dive headlong into a deep pool of clear water. Another was above the chicken house on the farm of my mother's parents. They kept hogs fenced in there and protected from the weather by the protruding rock which as I recall bore a constant drip, drip, drip of water. As a child when I saw and heard the dripping water, I thought of Jenny Wiley's escape from her captors near Mud Lick Falls. While the Indians were away hunting, they had left her bound and alone. She rolled herself to the edge of the rock house's overhanging rock roof to let the water drop onto her leather bindings to loosen them.

I imagined my stories emanating from the rock house I saw through the glass. It carried me to the past each Sunday morning long enough that I could recall stories that might bring my children closer to my past and their heritage and help them become acquainted with their people.

In those early days of my writing, I would listen to soft music.

WKLW in Paintsville broadcasts Dick Clark's *Rock Roll and Remember* every Sunday morning. Those classic sixties songs helped to carry me back to the days when my grandparents were alive. Music never interferes with my writing. Instead it lends a rhythm and helps transform my desk chair into, as Stephen King calls it, a "far-seeing place."

I was first in my class at Johnson Central High School in 1971 and would have been first in my class to throw my graduation cap sky high had this been tradition. I was anxious to leave, not only Johnson Central but the town of Paintsville as well. Since I had not really been anywhere, I believed my hometown to be the most stifling place in the world. I had been planning my escape to central Kentucky for a while and was ready to leave. I seldom went back. My only return visits were to attend Apple Festival concerts. There is no theatre or convention center in Johnson County so the high school gymnasium and stage are the setting for concerts every Apple Festival Saturday night. A walk down the main corridor to the restroom would take me close to the upper-floor classroom wings, but a glance through the hallway door window always brought me closer to my high school years and memories than I really wanted to be.

I enjoyed much of my own high school teaching years at the beginning of my career, but once I began teaching in college, I thought my days of walking through the noisy halls into a high school classroom and experiencing the energy level of sixteen-year-old students was over—WRONG!

My first experience teaching a college class on a high school campus came soon after I was hired when I was told that I would be teaching a night class at Sheldon Clark High School in Martin County. I was the latest hired and so of course the first chosen to make the drive over the mountains. Once I started teaching the course, I actually did not mind the drive or the pain of begging the janitors to let me into the building and classroom. I had several outstanding students. Few were still in high school. Most were taking classes on the Prestonsburg campus too and had taken this class in Inez to avoid a nighttime winter weather drive. One male student in his thirties was a member of the Martin County Board of Education and when the class ended in early May, offered me a job if I ever decided to return to high school teaching. I did not yet have tenure and was pleased to receive the offer.

I have learned never to say "never." In my twenty-eighth year of teaching I was once again called on to travel to a high school to teach a college course. This time would be different though. I was to teach an afternoon class at my old high school. Dual credit courses taught by high school faculty had evolved into college-only credit courses taught from our campus via interactive tele media and finally into transfer courses taught on high school campuses by college professors.

Things had changed, and things had stayed the same. The first change I noticed was a result of crimes committed on high school campuses across the nation and the tragic loss of life on September 11, 2001. Two uniformed security guards sat in eight-by-ten guardhouses. One was located to the left of the building's entrance between the school and the gated entrance to a McDonald's parking lot. This parking lot and restaurant are a part of Mayo Plaza shopping center. When I began my sophomore year here in 1968, the school was new. It was the only building on this stretch of Route 23. In my day the only "bootlegged" food in the building came from the oldest fast-food restaurant still serving—Dairy Queen, which was hardly within walking distance. Someone had to sneak a car off campus to make the food run with list in hand clearly noting who had ordered the onion rings, foot-long hot dogs with slaw, and peanut butter milkshakes.

Development of stores, banks, and restaurants continues near the plaza. Downtown Paintsville is virtually a ghost town today—replaced by a Super Wal-Mart. The other guardhouse restricts entry to the side parking lot reserved for teachers. A middle school, the board of education office, athletic fields, and a newer one-story brick building housing dressing rooms, a few classrooms, and an Olympic-sized swimming pool share the same entrance. The Golden Eagle football field is located behind the swimming pool building with the lighted baseball field nearby.

Upon entering the building that first Tuesday afternoon, I began having flashbacks. I wondered whether I was in the year 2002 or 1968. Students looked older than I remembered when I was a high school teacher. They were loud and walked in couples. Some were paired off in secluded corners.

Teachers appeared *younger* than I recalled them looking when I was a student. Don't laugh. I know the reason. I knew the reason before I ever saw them for the first time, but there are some things in life we just don't want to admit until we have to. The English classroom where I was to teach was the room of a former college student of mine, Karla McCarty. She greeted me with a familiar smile. This was her planning period, but she gave it up to make me feel comfortable and make sure I had what I needed to begin my class. I knew that she was looked upon as "old" by these students and realized I must appear ancient.

The old blackboard was well worn with age. There was an Internet-connected computer for the teacher's use. The windows had been replaced with more modern ones. Those were the only physical changes. Outside in the hallway, the lockers looked the

183

same. They were soon to be covered with banners that celebrated school spirit and students' support for their football team as it took on their principal rival, the Paintsville Tigers.

By returning to teach at my old high school I was hoping to give something back. So many teachers, long since retired, had been kind to me here—had given me the encouragement I needed to go on to college. Many of these teachers had been first-generation college students themselves. We may have lived in different parts of the county, and some of us had more than others, but we were all basically country kids from a community where our parents as well as our neighbors and teachers looked out for us. My own teachers must have felt they were giving back when they became teachers. This "giving back" business is instilled in us at a young age. I don't remember the class in which it was taught, but there must have been one. It was probably just prior to the class that taught us to appreciate what our parents sacrificed for us in order to encourage us to do the same for them when they became older.

The first of my students I recognized was Jacob. His mother was the daughter of a retired colleague of mine, Gus Kalos. Gus was professor of music at Prestonsburg Community College for many years. He was hired at the college's inception and was teaching there while I was still a JCHS band student participating in a regional band program at the college. The entire five-county region the college served knew of his successful program and outstanding teaching. I recalled seeing Gus picking up his grandchildren, Jacob among them, from Porter Elementary where my wife taught first grade. Where had the years gone?

Jessica was the second student I recognized. I saw her mother Carolyn in her. Carolyn had begun kindergarten teaching in Gallatin County where my wife and I began our careers. A few years into her career she met and married a man from Floyd County and moved to the mountains to continue her teaching career. I remembered feeling jealous of the fact that she had the opportunity to move to the mountains to teach before I did.

Lauren sat behind Jacob. She favored her mother Susie who had been hired to teach Spanish at JCHS. She was one year ahead of me in school and after graduating from Morehead State University had come home to take the place of our beloved Spanish teacher, Mr. Lagos. Teaching influences young people who may carry that influence on to others— generations removed.

One of college teaching's toughest challenges is building a sense of community in the classroom. The older the students the more those students are determined to remain in a protective cocoon that they have built for themselves. This barrier has proven effective in the past, isolating them from others and hiding similarities in life experiences that might have brought them closer to one another. I was surprised to find that a community already existed in my group of high school students. Many had known each other since grade school, and a community had been formed over time.

I remembered this sense of community from my own days at JCHS. We had stayed closest to students we had known from one of the four county grade schools. Our family began with shared experiences in the early grades, and memories of these experiences stayed with us through our junior high years and into high school. We were open to adopting others into our community and readily did so even if the students came from across the county several miles away. When one male student Jodi Mullins from Oil Springs School was badly hurt in a motorcycle accident, we joined to raise money at festivals to help his family pay the medical bills. When Tommie Lou Himes' sister and brother-in-law were killed in an automobile accident, we stood by her during her time of grief as if she were a member of our own families even though she was from Oil Springs too and had attended that school for eight years before we met her. I remember how sad we all felt the day she brought to school her sister's daughter, who was not with them in the accident. Tommie's parents had taken her in to raise. I should have expected that same sense of community not to have completely died, but as I said, years of college teaching had made discovering such a community unusual.

When my wife from central Kentucky began teaching here in east Kentucky, she immediately noticed a difference in the children. I will never forget what she said shortly after moving here. "The children are different here," she said. "They look out for each other. If one of them gets hurt on the playground, the others will try to take care of the hurt one. They will help the child inside the building and then worry about her or him until they are certain there is no cause for concern." I had explained this difference to her by telling her that these students were from a small community made up of country people who all were being brought up in the same manner. Their fathers were miners, farmers, or blue-collar workers in town like my father. Many were related to each other as I had been to several of my classmates at Flat Gap Elementary School and later at Johnson Central. When Tony Harris got in trouble in the boys' bathroom for taking out a bottle of whiskey along with a raw potato, taking a swig and then a bite of potato to chase it down, I remember feeling sad and worried about him. He was kin. He lived just down the graveled road from my papaw's farm, and we had played basketball on the dusty court near Alonzo's country store across from his parents' farm.

Another difference, I explained to my wife, was that in her part of Kentucky those who had moved there from other places such as Cincinnati or Louisville were not as close to their grandparents as were the children who attended Meade Memorial where she was teaching. Most of her students lived close to grandparents—probably *both* sets of grandparents—as had I. When I was growing up, my family's regular Sunday schedule included a short drive to my Slone grandparents' home for a chicken-and-dumpling dinner (what we now call lunch) complete with banana pudding for dessert. On our way home we would always stop at my mother's parents' farm where I would play with my cousin in and around one of the two barns and shoot baskets on a goal nailed to the side of one of the barns. As I look back now, my parents must have decided that Daddy's mother was the better cook because meals were most always eaten at their house whereas visiting was all that went on at my mother's parents' home.

Having such a close relationship with grandparents is like having two extra sets of parents to correct you when you are wrong or praise you when you deserve praise. Young people in the mountains who went bad had only themselves to blame because, they were taught right from wrong by a variety of teachers. Students whose families had migrated to the mountains from northern states caused most of the discipline problems. These were usually children who had been born into families who had migrated north for work. Their grandparents were still living on the home place back in Kentucky, close enough for twice-a-year visits but not every-Sunday visits.

Discovering a community in my old high school should not have surprised me. My work to build this sense of community in the college classroom takes a long time and sometimes fails. I soon discovered that the other students in my high school group looked

187

out after one student in particular, T.J. She always wore a smile. I soon discovered the reason she was so taken care of by her classmates. She was a superior caretaker in her own right. A colleague of mine Robert Looney taught speech to many of these same students on Mondays and Wednesdays. She was always looking out for *him*—trying to help make his teaching easier. When students were to be on a different time schedule she would always send word by me to Mr. Looney so that he would know about the change. She had a caring heart. Her classmates knew this about her and returned the favor. She was treated as she had treated others during their time together.

Melissa Murphy and Tiffany Howard were senior stars on one of the best girls' basketball teams in the state. They were as close as sisters. When one read a paper aloud for peer review, the other *felt* the paper being read. They were there for each other in tough times of loss as well as in times of celebration. Little did I know, but Melissa felt as close as family to *me* as well. I took to class one day a tape recording of Garrison Keillor telling a story about falling down on stage prior to one of his performances. His point was that falling is a common experience to us all—one that *should* draw us all closer to each other. After I played the tape, I asked my students to write a journal entry about an embarrassing fall they had experienced. When finished, I asked whether they had written something that they were proud enough of to share by reading aloud. Melissa's hand went up immediately even though it was time for class to end—another difference I had found between teaching in college and teaching in high school. College students grow very impatient if the professor goes over time and will rattle papers and close their books to express their impatience. If these high school students were interested in something, they were unaware of the clock, and I often found myself teaching beyond the scheduled end of class. They were never impatient although most had academic team or athletic practices or other activities scheduled for after school. Melissa had written about falling on the playground at Porter Elementary. Her friends had taken her inside to be cared for by her teacher, my wife Debbie. Melissa had never forgotten how caring my wife had been to her. She cleaned her up and even went to the family resource center to get her some clothes to wear that were not torn. That evening when I told my wife about Melissa's story, she did not remember the fall. She has taught so many first and second graders through the years. She *did* remember Melissa and could tell me everything about her, but she had forgotten the incident that had stayed in Melissa's memory. I suppose even on that first day when I must have appeared to be a stern professor, she knew I was OK because after all, Mrs. Slone had married me!

Shared tragedies bring us all closer. I came to understand just why these students were close when Kristin Adams read her paper about an angel. Kristin was a dancer. She had danced on national championship teams coached by Jody Shepherd. Danielle Nicole Ward, a fellow dancer and member of the school dance team, died shortly after getting her driver's license. She lost control of her car on the twisting mountain road between Paintsville and Inez. Her car swerved into the path of an oncoming tanker truck. I remembered the tragedy, not because I knew the student, but because I had read two other papers about the accident and her death written by Johnson County students enrolled in my class on campus. In both papers was a description of the spot on the heater/ac unit located on the window side of her homeroom classroom. Danielle Nicole had sat there in the mornings before the first-period bell. Her friends remembered this after her death and placed a sign, which read, "No sitting here. This space is reserved for an angel." When I first began teaching my college class in the high school building, I noticed the metal heating/cooling unit, thought of Danielle Nicole, and wondered whether this might be the place where she had sat. I asked my students whether this was the spot, and they told me that it was in a different classroom and that the sign was still there almost four years after her death.

As I listened to Kristin read her paper about her friend's life and death, I noticed that her peers were listening like a family. The paper's title was "White Carnations With a Pretty Pink Bow." She took us through her experience of purchasing the flowers from a local Food City floral department. Kristin carried the carnations with her to the visitation, funeral, and graveside where they triggered memories—flashbacks of Danielle Nicole's personality.

Students who might not have had a death in the family were *forced* into the grieving process upon the death of their friend. Danielle Nicole's death turned them into a family. At Nicole's service, her mother hugged Nicole's friends one by one. When she hugged Kristin, Kristin felt the touch of a "mother."

Two other examples come to mind. In both cases I have used these as models. Josh Daniels wrote about his papaw. He framed the paper with his papaw's wonderful sense of humor. His papaw had taught him the lesson that life could be improved with laughter. Upon retirement Josh's grandfather had taken up the habit of scavenging. Not unlike Harlan Hubbard in his Johnboat scouring the Ohio River for usable items others had discarded, Josh's grandfather drove a rusted '80 Toyota Corolla up and down mountain back roads stalking anything he thought was worth something. He was not looking for aluminum cans that he could receive money for; he was simply looking for items to add to his personal collection. His prized possession picked up beside the road this way was a

Bubba Gump Shrimp hat that he had recovered and brought home for Josh's grandmother to launder. He hung it up and never wore it because he was afraid of losing it. *Forest Gump* was his favorite movie—especially the parts where Forest was running across the country. Josh's papaw would call for family to join him in watching the movie over and over again. He never grew tired of laughing at Forest Gump.

Josh described his papaw so clearly that readers felt they knew him. No one in my family ever displayed such a wonderful quirkiness and sense of humor, but that did not keep me from being able to imagine that such a character could be living on Route 40 near Boonescamp, Kentucky.

The last example of Josh's papaw's sense of humor and love for life came in the form of an anecdote about a little dog that he owned. Josh came home from school one afternoon to find his papaw holding his side in laughter. "Come in here, Joskie, and watch. I can make this dog pee!" Josh didn't know just what he would find as he walked into the room adjacent to the back porch. His grandfather had discovered that the dog had learned to recognize that he was about to be fed when he heard the sound of the door handle being turned. Most of this afternoon, Josh's grandfather had delighted himself with the game of rattling the door handle in order to get the dog excited. Once excited, the dog could not control its bladder, and so each time he would hear the sound, he would pee a little on the gray porch boards. Josh's grandmother had not caught the two in the act of playing this little game, or she would have stopped it long before Josh arrived home, So much the better, for Josh got another laugh from his papaw, another memory to store away, and a wonderful idea for a first paper in a college writing class. By listening to Verna Mae Slone's advice, Josh discovered that it's OK to write about papaws who pick up garbage from the side of the road and train dogs to pee on cue.

The second example paper came from the most unlikely source. Early in each semester I am busy teaching and getting to know names of my new students. Associating names with faces becomes more and more difficult as each year passes. I did, though, notice one student in particular and learn her name in a negative way. She sat in a front seat near the center of the classroom. As I taught, I scanned the classroom. This may sound strange, but after many years of teaching in the same room, I have a set of memories associated with seat locations. In the front and to my left usually sits a star student who is willing to answer questions whenever called on. Stacey, who will some day soon replace one of our retiring math professors, sat there. Brandon Gibson and Brandon Haley sat there during my literature class. They were former writing students who earned the highest grade on every paper they submitted. They are close friends—one will be an engineer, the other, a flagman at Willard Speedway near Grayson, Kentucky, will be a coach and teacher some day soon. They looked forward to being introduced to Kentucky writers and in turn introduced them to family members. When they talked with each other in class quietly, it was because they were reacting to what was being taught.

Barbara Chandler and Jan Cook sat in those same seats during the first class I taught for our college. Barbara was a successful real-estate agent, and Jan was the wife of a prominent local surgeon. Both loved to write creatively about their experiences as children growing up or about their more recent experience raising their own children. In one paper I remember Jan "leaned on the old water pump handle," her fingers almost freezing to the ice cold metal as she pumped water to carry from the pump to her home. She went on to the

University of Kentucky to write for Gurney Norman in a creative writing class. I'm sure he would remember some of her work even as I do today.

On the right side of the room and a few seats back in the row near the door sat Beverly Pruitt. She would always be seated in that location, regardless of the room. She was my only grandmother that semester, and I asked her to read when I brought to class a Cynthia Rylant children's book about growing up in Appalachia. She knew just how to pause and show the pictures as she waved the book slowly from side to side above her head for all to see. She remembered to flash the illustrations my way so that I could become her imaginary grandchild too.

In the back left corner will be two shy students who want to learn but *never* to be called on. They will be respectful of me and of their classmates, but they will never say a word in class or even on their way in or out the door. Seated in the opposite corner will often be a husband and wife. He will speak for them both, eagerly participating in class, but she will outperform him on all papers and tests. In the front of this row will be a mother and daughter—mother in front, of course, and when attendance is added up at the end of the term, the mother will have fewer absences than the daughter with whom she shares notes, pens, and paper. The daughter has not grown to accept responsibility.

This semester Tabatha sat in front of the second row from the door, and from her expression, I was certain she did so in order to make a quick escape if need be. Her look at once convinced me that she *hated* the college, the class, and *me*. Have I said that I am not *always* correct in my analysis though? If my mental map and my reading of faces were always correct, each class I would see the student seated in the back seat, center row. That is where a young lady sat who had enrolled in college to earn her degree in matrimony. Applying make-up always had priority over taking notes.

Thankfully I am wrong sometimes as I was in my evaluation of Tabatha. I discovered that, like Josh, she had listened to Verna Mae Slone say, "Don't write for anybody else. Write to please yourself and let them like it or not."

Tabatha wrote about her papaw—really about one particular day. She chose this day to represent all the days she spent with him. Since he had passed, this was the day she had kept with her as a symbol of their relationship. She could smell the twist of tobacco he took from his pocket for a chew. When she asked for some, he was quick to offer a bowl of homemade candy as a substitute. He could make her feel special with only a wink and a kind word.

I read Tabatha's paper to another class, and Kelley, seated in the dreaded marriage-major seat surprised me with her own "papaw" story. She recalled no specific day and time spent with her papaw, but instead most of her "dates" with her papaw. From the time she was old enough to remember, her papaw would take her to McDonald's. What made this "date" so special was that it would always be just the two of them. One day she convinced her papaw that she was grown-up enough to hold the money. Her papaw's old pick-up truck had no air conditioning, and so you can guess what happened to the wad of dollar bills she held in her hand when she had to do what all children do when riding in a truck with the window down. The money went flying out the window in the breeze. She remembered thinking her papaw would be angry with her. He was not mad at all as he reassured her they could still go on their "date." He had some more money tucked away for food. More recently something similar occurred, but this time more money was involved. Kelley wrecked her papaw's new black extended cab truck—his pride and joy. The truck was badly damaged, but Kelley would recover from her minor injuries. When her papaw came to see her in the hospital room, through tears he said the truck could be replaced but not his granddaughter.

I was reminded of writer, teacher, and Grundy, Virginia native Lee Smith's discovery that it was OK to write about her grandmother sitting on the front porch talking to one of her aunts about whether or not one of the two had colitis. She learned what all students need to learn. Writing doesn't have to be about exotic people and places. Students should write about their home place and the memories *their* people made there.

CHAPTER TWENTY-ONE

While always teaching writing classes at Big Sandy Community and Technical College, I often taught Spanish classes as well. When anyone asks how I became a Spanish major in college, I am quick to tell them and compliment my high school Spanish teacher, Raul Lagos, from Santiago, Chile, who inspired me to become a Spanish teacher. He and his wife came to teach in my home county in the fall of 1969, in a first-of-its-kind teacher exchange program between our country and his native country. The study of Spanish took me far away to places I had never been. I never grew tired of listening to Mr. Lagos talk about his native Chile. His eyes would widen when he would speak about his South American hero, the soccer player Pele. Mr. Lagos even started the school's first soccer team. The team practiced in the basketball gymnasium after school. There were no soccer fields in east Kentucky in 1969.

Those were the days when the mountains remained segregated and oblivious to what was occurring in the civil rights movement in other parts of the country. No African Americans lived inside the boundaries of my home county, nor did any Hispanics. Mr. Lagos and his wife were the only Hispanics most of us had seen except on TV. I had not traveled farther from home than Springfield, Ohio, where my mother's sister Doris lived, but I could travel every day in Spanish class. I loved listening to Mr. Lagos talk about *his* mountains located not far from the Chilean coast. He could swim in the ocean in the morning and drive to the mountains for skiing in the afternoon.

Mrs. Atha Stewart, librarian at Gallatin County High, where I began my teaching career thirty years ago, once told me that she believed something mysterious occurred after students began learning a foreign language. Their (English) writing abilities improved. Her daughter Mary Jane was a student of mine in both my Spanish and English classes. Mary Jane's improvement was but one example of many Miss Atha had observed over the years. Miss Atha began her own career by teaching first and second grades where her students loved her so much that they began calling her Miss Atha instead of Mrs. Stewart. She returned to graduate school in order to obtain her master's degree in library science and retired from her home county's school system—loved by every student who was blessed to have come under her influence.

Miss Atha's husband Clarence was a farmer who raised cattle and tobacco on a rolling-hills farm intersected by Interstate 71, northern Kentucky's new connecting route between Louisville and Cincinnati. I remember one of Mary Jane's essays, in which she remembered her family's farm before the arrival of the interstate highway. She contrasted the peacefulness of the farm before, to the constant drone of the highway traffic after 1978. The Stewarts were *connected* to the land, their church, their rural community, the county school, and Warsaw, the county seat. Miss Atha was an excellent librarian and teacher because she was happy outside the classroom first. She arrived at school happy in the morning and left happy in the afternoon. She taught young teachers, who would listen, that if they put God and family first, the rest of life including their teaching would take care of itself.

Neither Miss Atha nor I knew why studying a foreign language helps one become a better writer, but I soon began to notice the positive effect the study of Spanish had on students' writing myself. As I looked back on my own education, I realized Spanish had improved my writing skills too as well as my performance as a teacher of writing.

Mine was a double major of English and Spanish with certification to teach both. I chose a double major with the "politics" of obtaining a teaching position once I graduated from college in mind. I knew that with a double major including a foreign language that I would have a better chance of obtaining a teaching position without the aid of "political pull." Politics in education in the mountains had nothing to do with party affiliation. Politics meant "I will help you if you help me" relationships with those whom you and your family knew well (often since childhood) and with whom you all agreed concerning important local issues. School systems in rural Kentucky are often the largest employer in the county. Superintendents who found themselves on the wrong side of the political fence were soon without jobs. Young people whose family members opposed the power of local superintendents had no hope of being hired to teach.

My interest in the Spanish language began in my Spanish classes at Johnson Central High. Mountain schools were having a difficult time finding Spanish teachers. The best they could hope for in most cases was a candidate who had completed a minor in Spanish. Our school was new in 1968 and was built with a state-of-the art language lab. In order to find a teacher fluent in Spanish, the administration in the fall of 1969 decided to participate in a national teacher exchange program, which brought to Johnson County Mr. and Mrs. Raul Lagos from Santiago, Chile.

Mr. Lagos taught at my high school while his wife taught Spanish in the Paintsville Independent School system. Mr. and Mrs. Lagos stayed in east Kentucky through and beyond my graduation year of 1971. They eventually secured their permanent visas and moved to Lexington where he taught Spanish at Henry Clay High, and she became the coordinator of foreign language instruction for the Fayette County Public School system. What a benefit it was for me to come under the influence of a native Spanish speaker and an excellent teacher! I not only learned the language; I learned about the Chilean culture and politics as well.

Mr. and Mrs. Lagos felt almost as if they were hiding in refuge in the east Kentucky mountains during these years of turbulence in their native Chile. In 1970, socialist Salvador Allende assumed power, and his dictatorship lasted until he was assassinated in 1973 during a military coup. While he was in power, the government took over industries such as the copper mines and oil companies. Chilean citizens lost the democratic rights they had struggled to gain through the sixties. Although Mr. and Mrs. Lagos missed their families terribly, they enjoyed the freedom of living in the United States. They were in awe of the freedom of speech here we take for granted. They watched Viet Nam War protests on the national news in disbelief. They had never had the freedom to express themselves on national political issues.

I remember Mr. Lagos as one of those teachers who, if they saw a spark of talent in one of their students, would not let that student do second-rate work. After I graduated from high school, he let me know that he *expected* me to teach Spanish some day. I hope he found out that I went on to teach high school Spanish for nine years and college Spanish for ten years at Prestonsburg Community College as well as at Alice Lloyd College in Pippa Passes.

I carried Mr. Lagos' influence on my pronunciation into college and into the Spanish classes I taught. The best example was the way I pronounced the *ll* and *y* in Spanish. Most Spanish texts and teachers encourage new speakers to pronounce *ll* as if it were a normal English *y*. I pronounce them as he taught me—with the Chilean pronunciation, *zsh*. We would record our spoken Spanish on tapes at our desks and then listen to ourselves on headphones. We were quite technologically sophisticated for 1969.

In his last years in education, Mr. Lagos became an assistant principal. I hope he never had to give up the teaching of Spanish, but if he did, his teaching survives today in another of his pupils, Susie Preston Greer, who teaches Spanish to my daughter Beth. Beth even pronounces the *y* sound in the pronoun *yo* (I) just as Mr. Lagos did—with the Chilean *zsh* sound. I'm certain that Mrs. Greer thinks of Mr. Lagos often as she carries on the tradition he began at Johnson Central High when the school was new and when he himself was a newcomer to our country. I know he was with me as I taught Spanish and that knowledge of the syntax of a second language has helped my students become better writers as it has helped me to be a better writing teacher just as Miss Atha told me it would almost thirty years ago.

When I began teaching Spanish, I called Susie Greer to find out about the texts and materials she used. She had been teaching one year longer than I. I assumed correctly that she was using the same publishing company that Mr. Lagos had used. My daughter tells me that Mrs. Greer has not lost the enthusiasm for teaching Spanish that I heard reflected in her voice back in the fall of 1975. While serving as an administrator at our college, I had the chance to hire Mrs. Greer to teach evening classes as an adjunct. She did an excellent job as always.

While teaching college Spanish myself, I had the chance to do some experimenting that I'm sure Mr. Lagos would have loved to have tried himself. Working with the public schools gifted and talented programs, I opened my college classroom to sixth grade students by providing them the opportunity to audit my college Spanish classes. These age eleven girls and boys sat alongside college students ranging in age from eighteen to forty-five. Although they were auditing the course, they were required to complete every activity and exam others in the class were required to complete. It was a little unusual at first to dismiss a college class only to find parents waiting proudly outside the door to pick up their sons daughters. I found myself having parent conferences every day. Parents were anxiously interested in how their children were doing. I never had to deliver a negative report.

I discovered what I had always believed to be true. Foreign language is best learned at an early age before old habits become ingrained and before there is any fear of embarrassment in sounding foolish when attempting to speak the target language. My sixth graders without exception did well. Their eagerness to learn to *speak* Spanish was especially infectious. They charged the classroom with a level of energy seldom found in a college class. The older we become the more barriers we put up against trying something new. Those eleven year olds were not afraid at all. Older students did better than the little ones only on written tests. Older college students had a great deal more experience taking tests and through high school and other college classes had become quite expert in the art of taking exams. The sad truth is that they had also learned to value grades more than the thrill of learning for learning's sake my young students still enjoyed. Each day I teach, I struggle to convince students to learn for the excitement of learning itself when they have been conditioned to learn only in order to receive a grade.

I found myself taking care of my new younger students in ways I was not used to doing with my older students, and I discovered that my older college students were doing the same as I. Each sixth grade student was "adopted" by a traditional or non-traditional college student who became teachers themselves. They sat beside the children and helped them when they needed extra attention or reinforcement. I imagined what I saw occurring must have been the forming of the same sort of learning community that existed in the east Kentucky one-room school.

In later years I again taught some of these same students as regular college freshmen or sophomores. Without fail they come up to me after class to tell me they will never forget their first college class with me. I'm glad I had the opportunity, much the same as the Kentucky Governor's Scholar program provides today, to give pre-college students a taste of the excitement of learning a college class can provide.

At the end of my own junior year of college at Eastern Kentucky University, Dr. Clarkson, my Spanish professor, convinced me that if I intended to teach Spanish, I should immerse myself in the Hispanic culture by traveling and studying in Mexico along with a group of students. The majority of my stay was to be in Mexico City where we stayed at Hotel Sevilla, a small hotel that most tourists did not know about. Dr. Clarkson's wife was from Mexico City. Her grandmother still lived there. He traveled there each summer regardless of whether he took a group of students along for a study tour. Thanks to his experience in Mexico, our tour and stay would cost less than one thousand dollars each, including money for meals.

I knew I did not have the money for the four-week stay in Monterrey, Puebla, Mexico City, and Acapulco. On the cover of my poetry collection, *At Home in the Mountains*, is a watercolor painting of a pinwheel-patterned quilt hanging on a clothesline. When I see this painting, I think of my mother's sacrifice so that I could afford to travel and study in Mexico. She worked quilting quilts with her signature, perfectly straight and evenly spaced zigzag stitch and saved most of the money I needed to travel with the EKU group. One bedroom in our rented house was kept empty of any furniture so that my mother could get down on hands and knees to measure and mark in pencil, using one side of an old quilting frame, the lines for her stitches. She would assemble the lining, the Mountain Mist padding, and the pieced quilt top on the bare wood floor. The window she kept curtainless to better illuminate her work. After quilting, she would wash the quilt and (She never owned a clothes dryer) allow it to dry on a poplar limb propped clothesline similar to the one in Tom Whitaker's painting. "On the Line" is the only one of Tom's prints that I keep hanging on my wall both in my office on campus and in my home. It is a constant reminder of a sacrifice I will never forget.

To save money our group drove to Mexico in two college vans instead of flying. My fellow travelers probably did not realize, but the trip *itself* was an education for me. I had never been farther away from home than the neighboring states of Ohio or West Virginia. I had the chance to see Dallas, Houston, New Orleans, and many other cities I had never visited. I had never seen deserts with mountains in the distance. I had never seen trees so short they looked more like bushes. Near the end of our stay, I clearly remember missing family most of all, home cooking a close second, and last but not least, I missed Kentucky's trees and the deep early summer shade of green only found in the mountains of east Kentucky.

Some lessons are best learned by stepping away for a time and then returning. That is a good way to describe my study tour in Mexico and the lessons I gleaned from my stay there. I learned Spanish words I had never learned in classes. I saw my first shadowy Van Gogh painting in the National Museum of Art. Seated on concrete benches among ninety thousand screaming fans, I saw my first soccer match in the Estadio Azteca. I rode the gondolas in the canals of Xochimilco, saw the Ballet Folklorico in the Palacio de Bellas Artes, and climbed the pyramids of Teotihuacan.

I learned that there were similarities between the Mexican culture and my own. For example, I realized the importance placed on faith as I watched pilgrims crawl on hands and knees across the square and up the steps into the Basilica de Guadalupe. They "prayed the steps" to receive God's blessing and answers to their prayers. On one wall inside the church was a mural depicting the Virgin Mary, appearing in a vision to a peasant, with instructions for the church to be built in this location.

I learned about the Mexican economy as I listened to my cab driver as he explained his belief that all Americans were rich because our dollar was worth so much more than the peso. Then I understood why Americans were targets for inflated prices. The widely held belief was that money came so easy for us that we would not miss a few dollars here or there. I saw the very wealthy living not so far away from the poor the same as in my home state. I met residents of the city who, like my great grandparents in the Kentucky mountains, had never traveled any farther from their homes than a few miles during their lifetimes. In Cuernavaca and in Taxco, I saw a love and appreciation for the beauty of flowers. Bright colored flowers were planted in makeshift "pots" and placed all along every balcony just as my mamaw Slone used to do.

I saw signs on the Universidad Autonoma Metropolitana

(UNAM—University of Mexico) campus protesting America's involvement in Mexican and Central American politics and felt hated and afraid because of my government's actions. For the first time, I was able to see ourselves as others saw us.

By immersing myself in another culture, I was able to discover contrasts and similarities between the Mexican culture and my own. Appalachian artists and writers understand that their best supporters are often those transplanted from the mountain culture who, because they have moved away, have a better perspective on the value of their roots. An appreciation for one's cultural heritage is sadly sometimes possible only from a distance. I came home with more than a knowledge of Mexico, its language, and its people. I also returned with a better appreciation and understanding of my *own* culture. Thanks, Dr. Clarkson, for teaching me more than you realized and thank you, Mom, for quilting the quilts that made my travel possible.

My high school Spanish years were during the Viet Nam era of course, and many of us had brothers or other relatives who were overseas in the military. If we were not related to anyone in Viet Nam, we knew of someone who was. The east Kentucky mountains have been a place resistant to change but also a place where loyalty to our nation and our government has remained strong. We saw the riots and protests on the nightly news, but none of the protests ever came from the mountains of east Kentucky. We did not question our country's involvement in the "police action" – war. We believed that to disagree with our government would be to fail to support our neighbors and our kin serving in the military. The idea of questioning our involvement in another country's affairs never occurred to us.

At the time, I did not realize that, in addition to his excellent teaching, the influence of Mr. Lagos' political beliefs would remain with me today. He would not stray from the lesson often, but the nature of teaching a foreign language calls for discussion of cultural and political differences. Mr. Lagos was alone in his beliefs, which emanated from a more objective perspective. He believed our country had no business being involved in the war between North and South Viet Nam. The argument that we were saving the world from the spread of communism was not a valid one to him because, if that was our mission, we had long ago failed in his native Chile. We were too embedded in our cocoon of patriotism, support for our troops, and naiveté. We nevertheless respected his opinion and did not let his views distract us from our study of Spanish. We could have learned so much more from him than the Spanish language if we had been open and ready to receive.

Students need to be *ready* to learn. Kindergarten and first-grade teachers understand this fact that I have only recently learned. I suspect I am not alone. Mr. Lagos was at a destination in his thinking where we students were not ready to travel. No matter how much he wanted us to learn from his more objective viewpoint, we were not ready to receive. Teachers must be aware that they may be at a point in their thinking that their students have not yet reached. The best teacher cannot reach students if they are not ready to be reached. Students are not always ready to receive, as I was not during my junior year of high school in 1969. I could memorize vocabulary for quizzes and mimic pronunciation, but I was not far enough along in the development of my critical thinking skills to accept evidence that might disprove everything I had learned up to this point from my other teachers, my relatives, and friends.

Soon after I stopped teaching Spanish at Big Sandy Community and Technical College, I received a phone call from Richard Kennedy, a division chair at Alice Lloyd College located in Pippa

Passes in Knott County, Kentucky. He wanted to know whether I could drive to Knott County to teach two Spanish classes for his college on a part-time basis. I said yes because I had heard good things about the students there. Saying yes to opportunities to teach students who want to learn is always an easy choice. The most rewarding teaching experiences occur while teaching students who love learning. The most unrewarding teaching experiences occur when students are forced to attend.

This unscientific observation, comes from one person's experiences, but take a look at those experiences before making judgment. When I taught in Gallatin County, parents would say to me, "Do what you can with my son/daughter. I can't do anything with him/her at home, and the courts have ordered my child to stay in school or be put in jail." These young people were the small percentage who made teaching difficult. No success stories come from forced attendance.

The other *forced* attendance situation I often saw while teaching secondary was the one in which students had been told by their parents that they could drop out of school as soon as they were sixteen, the legal drop-out age in Kentucky at that time. These students seldom attended unless forced to by the pupil personnel director, Gordon Hendrix, and Mr. Hendrix had his hands full.

The job pool in northern Kentucky in the late seventies and early eighties was a good one. Florence, Kentucky, located in Boone County, the neighboring county to the north only ten miles south of Cincinnati, was a booming industrial center for the greater Cincinnati area complete with the growing Cincinnati International Airport located in the same county in nearby Hebron. Migration out of Gallatin County for work in Boone County reminded me of the Great Migration out of the mountains of east Kentucky during the forties and fifties. Many of my students were a part of this northern Kentucky migration. Gallatin County students knew that factory jobs required little formal education and saw no need for education beyond the basic math and reading skills required to get a job. Teachers faced quite a challenge teaching young people in northern Kentucky who had no plans to stay and graduate.

The opportunity to teach at Alice Lloyd College, where the students wanted preparation for professions that required a four-year degree or beyond, was one that I could not let pass by.

As I drove down Route 80, the newer four-lane highway connecting Prestonsburg with Hazard, I remembered the twisting old road that this new highway had replaced. "I have never ridden on such a crooked road in my life," I remember thinking while riding along with my father who was taking a load of tires to service stations along the way between Prestonsburg and Hindman. I thought that this new four-lane must surely be the "broad highway" Knott County's James Still traveled often and wrote about in his poem, "White Highways":

> *I have seen the hills pushed back*
> *and bridges thrust across rivers....*

There is only one exit for Hindman, Kentucky. Soon after taking it and passing through the town, I found myself on one of the small roads Mr. Still preferred. His beloved Hindman Settlement School was on my right as I drove on toward Pippa Passes. Luckily I had learned to drive on roads like these. I saw my surname everywhere: on storefronts, mailboxes, repair shops, billboards advertising candidates for local political offices, etc. I knew that more Slones lived here than in any Kentucky county and that the descendants of Little Granny Alice Slone had once been permitted to attend Alice

Lloyd College free of tuition because the land where the college was situated was given to Mrs. Lloyd by the Slone family.

The campus was situated deep in a valley beside a quiet, meandering stream. Most buildings were painted brown. The old founders' cabin had been sided in board and batten style, to duplicate the old simple mountain style of home building. I felt at home.

My class was in one of the newer brick buildings that housed the art gallery and the auditorium where Tuesday convocations were held. Along the hallway to my classroom, I noticed piano practice rooms and a chorus room and band room. Mr. Kennedy, my division chair, was the music professor. He toured the country with the famous Alice Lloyd College choir. Once inside his office, students greeted me. Every student at the college is required to work a specified number of hours each week in order to remit tuition. I learned quickly that without student employment, the college could not function. Students did everything from running the college radio station, WWJD, a Christian music and information station, to driving the end loaders that kept Caney Creek from overflowing its boundaries. The campus was a little world of its own. Students, staff, and faculty ate together at what was called the "Hunger Din," the school's cafeteria. I was offered a meal ticket myself and encouraged to eat supper there after my classes were over.

My two Spanish classes were made up of an eclectic group of young people, except for one lady in her thirties. I learned that even my one non-traditional student was required to work on campus to defray tuition. She said that she had been willing to pay because she also had a job off campus, but she had not been permitted to do so. Her job was in the day care, caring for the children of faculty and staff. There was a high school located on campus, the June Buchanan School. Housing was provided not only for students but for faculty as well. New faculty lived in older apartments while senior faculty had graduated to housing that resembled modern condominiums that could be found in city suburbs. Mr. Kennedy told me he was investing in his retirement home and had it nearly paid for because he had never paid a mortgage for his housing on the campus.

I discovered on the first day of classes that one of my students was from my home county, Johnson County. When she introduced herself to me, I learned that she was the granddaughter of the owners of a small house my father had rented where we had lived while I was in high school. She was named Georgina after her grandmother, Georgine. Her grandfather was Howard Dills. I had last seen her mother Mabel with my new Spanish student in her arms—a baby not yet one year old. Mabel's marriage had failed, and she and her baby daughter had returned to live with Mabel's parents. Georgine Dills ran a country store that was located beside our house. Actually there was a toilet between the two buildings. Tom's Creek ran behind all three.

I never mention outdoor toilets from my past in my writing because I hate them to this day. I do so here only because I remember it better than my own room in the little house, built on stilts to avoid flash flooding from Tom's Creek. I became sixteen there, a self-conscious age and was keenly aware that most of my friends not only had color TVs but indoor bathrooms as well. I remember wishing that we lived in a trailer instead so that we would have a bathroom and I would not have to risk being seen by peers carrying the wire baled handle of the white and red, lidded chamber pot to the toilet and back. I still recall sitting inside the unpainted toilet staring through the cracks at people I knew who were going in and out of Georgine's store. I hoped they did not see me go in and waited to leave until they were inside the store or in their cars driving away.

The parking area was graveled, so I could hear an approaching car before I could see it through the cracks in the door, and that helped me avoid many embarrassing encounters.

Upstairs over the store was an apartment likewise with no indoor plumbing. The lady who lived there emptied their dishwater over the banister on the back porch and into the creek below. Once when I was walking there beneath the porch, the lady did not quite reach the creek with the dishpan's contents. I was drenched! She heard my scream, realized what she had done, and was embarrassed but not as much I was. On that walk home, I did not take the time to worry whether or not I had an audience.

Seeing Georgine's granddaughter in my class brought back memories. My head was as if soaked with them. I suppose we all have flashbacks of where we *were* as opposed to where we *are* in life. I get these as I drive by places we lived and recall times when we were poor—when all I had were dreams.

Now as I teach, I recognize at once whether students have dreams of their own. Some family member may have instilled in them the idea that their dreams can come true. If not, I try to show the student the importance of setting goals and striving to achieve them—the only way out of poverty I know of and the one I know from personal experience.

Georgine's granddaughter was living out her dream, a dream encouraged by her mother and grandmother. She disliked the vocabulary quizzes I gave but was an outstanding student and a hard worker both in and out of the classroom. I am sure she is successful today teaching students of her own, and I hope she teaches them a little Spanish along the way. My Spanish teachers would be happy to hear of this too because they must have realized before I did that this teaching business is like the passing of a baton in a relay race. If the pass is completed successfully from teachers to students, they may, in turn, become teachers themselves and pass the baton along.

I enjoyed the experience of teaching at Alice Lloyd College. I saw students who were given responsibilities *along with* educational opportunities. As a result traditional-aged students gained maturity more quickly than is usually the case on a larger university campus where students do not feel they need to grow up and become a part of a community like the community of students at Alice Lloyd College.

CHAPTER TWENTY-TWO

I taught in northern Kentucky with a variety of folks from a wide range of backgrounds. People whose parents moved to a place from somewhere else and people who themselves migrated to an area are not deeply rooted to their place. A major industrial center like northern Kentucky has more transplants than small towns and rural areas. I can trace my ancestors in the mountains back to John Slone who came to my part of east Kentucky in search of cheap land to farm around 1850, from Scott County, Virginia. He found the land he wanted and traded the saddle from the horse he rode in on for the 200 acres that the home place still stands on today.

One of those who had moved to Gallatin County from another place was Doug Aulick. Like many of us in those early days of our teaching careers, Doug liked to experiment with his teaching. He was from one of those old German neighborhoods in Covington, Kentucky, where a European sense of community survived. Neighbors watched out for each other and especially for the children. He remembered block parties and festival-like community celebrations before the days of Oktoberfests and other German heritage festivals. Doug missed that sense of community not present in Gallatin County. With the approval of the superintendent, Jim Wallace, who was looking for a way to improve public community relations, Doug started the tradition of parent/student exchange day.

Students were permitted to stay home if one of their parents or grandparents agreed to attend school in their place.

I remember this experiment well because it was the first time I ever taught someone older than I. Not all parents participated, so classes were made up of an interesting mixture of young people, parents, and grandparents. Teachers were to go about their teaching as usual, and we did so as best we could. One exception was when a feature reporter from WLWT TV came to my door to ask if she could video my class of adults and teens. I lost total grasp of the Spanish verbs I was teaching. My students became nervous and pretty much illiterate as well. Thank God for voiceovers and video editing.

This parent/student exchange lasted one day out of a long school term, but it did improve community relations. Criticizing became much more difficult once adults had experienced the environment and classroom instruction first-hand or at least had heard about the experience from someone with more courage who had participated in the exchange. Doug Aulick's experiment taught me that inviting members of the community to class could foster a positive relationship between the school and the community it serves.

Big Sandy Community and Technical College serves a five-county area in the Big Sandy Valley. Enough of our alumni have gone on to finish their degrees and return to enrich the community that we do not have the same problem with public relations, as did the Gallatin County school system. My family's doctor and dentist earned degrees from our college before transferring to complete their study. Still, inviting community members to one of our campuses accomplishes the same goal that the student/parent exchange did by keeping our doors open and allowing the communities we serve to know what we do inside our buildings.

One Wednesday evening I climbed the stairs to the second floor of our Pikeville classroom building to find our presenter for the night engrossed in conversation with my students seated in the foyer. She barely noticed the teacher had arrived and that she was in danger of being late for her presentation. I interrupted by introducing myself to her.

Ms. Georgiana Muncy was 98 pounds of boundless energy. Her eyes sparkled from behind her contemporary herringbone-frame glasses. Beside her rested a cloth bag containing her "mysteries." She took a seat next to her old and newfound friends. As it turned out, she knew many of my students—remembered them when they were small or if she had forgotten, had just been reminded by them that they had met one another on one of her visits to their schools. She reminded me of Ms. Van Horn, who came to my little country grade school, Flat Gap, to teach Bible lessons. The separation of church and state that forbade Bible lessons and prayer in school had had no impact at Flat Gap Elementary. No one complained because Ms. Van Horn taught across all denominations. Like Ms. Muncy, she always brought along visual aids. She would unfold a black felt board and unpack stick-on words and characters that soon came to colorful life. Sometimes she brought puppets or stuffed animals as well.

Ms. Muncy resembled Ms. Van Horn in other ways too. She had the same easy, soft-spoken manner. From her cloth bag she began to pull out the characters that would appear in her stories, for she was a mountain storyteller. She had attended national conferences like the annual storytelling convention in Jonesborough, Tennessee, and had traveled nationwide, sharing her talent and learning from other storytellers as well. Lately she had been speaking to teachers' groups, encouraging young teachers to use her story-telling techniques in order to make children's literature come alive and to inspire mountain

215

children to continue the Appalachian oral tradition. As she introduced herself to my students, she mentioned storytellers they had heard of as well as local writers who had garnered a national reputation. Through her job as a local librarian she had met such famous authors as Dr. Leonard Roberts and James Still. She loved the folk music and singing of the internationally known singer and songwriter, Jean Ritchie from Perry County. She played for them a cassette sampling of Jean Ritchie's music and singing.

Ms. Muncy's first story was "Tale of a 'Possum." It was a tale about trust, told from the point of view of a 'possum whose personality resembled Ms. Muncy's. The 'possum had some unfortunate encounters with one Mr. Snake, and Ms. Muncy reveled in changing voices and personalities as she spoke the dialogue of *both* the characters in her story through puppets. She especially enjoyed performing the hissing voice of the snake—mixing in his words here and there. We saw her lose herself in her story. She *became* the characters in her story.

Ms. Muncy's next story was a "true" ghost tale about a man who had the habit of visiting cemeteries and encouraging skeletons in graves to rise up and talk. We all realized how popular ghost stories are to children and could just imagine the terrible joy in the expressions on children's faces as they opened up their imaginations enough to just maybe *believe* the story was true.

We were afraid that Ms. Muncy was nearing the end of her presentation, and so I asked her to talk about some of the handmade toys that she had brought to class. One was a wooden paddle dancer. She demonstrated it by tapping the paddleboard against her knee causing a wooden man, dressed in bibbed overalls to dance. She called its dance a shuffle dance and asked whether my students had seen such a dance performed by a person. A few had as had I at

Bluegrass music festivals. Some had not though, so this seventy-something lady stepped forward to demonstrate. She challenged my students to join her, and to my surprise, a few did step up in front of the class to shuffle dance alongside her. As she lost *herself* in her stories, she caused these students to lose all fear of appearing foolish by dancing in front of a group!

Former teachers who miss the classroom become excellent presenters. One such former teacher is Meredith Slone who visited my Appalachian literature class to share his love for making and playing dulcimers. Mr. Slone taught for twenty-seven years, some of them in the last surviving one-room school in Kentucky. Mr. Slone's interest in dulcimers began when he saw Jean Ritchie perform at Alice Lloyd College.

When Mr. Slone was in junior high his fingertip was cut off in an accident, so he could not chord a guitar. The dulcimer can be chorded with a wooden rod or with one forefinger in the style Mr. Slone preferred. He learned to play the instrument by ear. His strong desire to play came while he was a young man living and working in Detroit. The music helped to cure his homesickness for the mountains.

The first song Mr. Slone performed on our campus in the spring of 2004 was "Wildwood Flower," the first song he had learned to play by ear. This particular song seems to live in the air in the mountains. Its traditional melody has been passed down through the generations.

Meredith Slone has been making dulcimers for the past thirty-seven years since he learned the craft from Charlie Whitaker, who taught at Alice Lloyd College. Every dulcimer he has made has its own unique story. The first one he showed to my students he called "Missed Opportunity." All his dulcimers have unique hand-carved designs. On this one the shapes of turkeys had been carved into the walnut top. While turkey hunting in the woods near his home, Mr. Slone had been scared into missing the bird by a rattlesnake. Although he missed the turkey, he did shoot the snake. He shook the dulcimer so that we could hear the snake's rattles that he had placed inside the dulcimer to remind him of the story.

Mr. Slone has donated his dulcimers to charities where they have been auctioned for more than a thousand dollars apiece; however, he has never sold a dulcimer for more than eighty-five dollars in his life. He explained that if he had to buy the wood from a lumber store, the wood itself would cost more than forty dollars. Instead he uses the walnut, poplar, or cherry he harvests from the forest. When asked why he charges only eighty-five dollars for each dulcimer he makes, he said that he wanted his dulcimers to be in the hands of ordinary people, people who might have to save a while just to acquire the money to buy the instrument. He did not want his dulcimers to be the home decor of wealthy people. He wanted them to be played by children of working-class mountain families.

One of the oldest dulcimers he brought to class that day had been broken and repaired several times. The reason was that Mr. Slone had loaned it to students through the years. When it would be returned broken, he would never become angry with the child. He had permitted the student to take the dulcimer home because he had seen a spark of interest. The value of getting the instrument into the hands of a child who might learn to play was far more important than the value of the dulcimer itself. So if it came back broken, he repaired it and then loaned it once again. He was proud of the instrument's imperfections, which had become symbols of its use.

My student who researched the dulcimer and invited Mr. Slone to present sat in front of the class alongside him as he performed and told his stories. Shannon Payne is from Jacksonville, Florida. She had researched the instrument and expressed her interest in the performer by sitting alongside Mr. Slone in front of the class. Mr. Slone decided to include Shannon in his performance. This was the first time she had ever seen a dulcimer in person or heard one played.

Mr. Slone brought out what he called his "courting dulcimer." After giving Shannon a brief lesson, Mr. Slone and Shannon sat face-to-face holding the double dulcimer on their laps between them. This "courting dulcimer" had two necks extending in opposite directions. It was really two dulcimers joined into one so that a young man and his sweetheart could play the instrument together. The name came from the design of the instrument, which allowed the couple to be porch-swing close to one another. In fact as they played, their knees touched! We all recognized the version of "Mary Had a Little Lamb." Even though Shannon had never held a dulcimer before, we could see how much fun she had trying to play. Shannon and her classmates appreciated Meredith Slone's passion for performing and making dulcimers.

My students have respect for community members like Ms. Muncy and Mr. Slone who take time from their lives to present to my class. As I have reviewed the notes they have taken, I see that students have not just learned about Appalachian culture. Many say how much both presenters *enjoyed* what they were doing. Maybe some of them will be inspired to take pride in doing what *they* enjoy through their own careers.

Something needs to be said again here not only about the importance of using local community resources in the classroom but also about the importance of *letting go*. So many of my own teachers could not release control. I copied their teaching style during the beginning of my career out of fear of failure. I do not consider teachers who stand

and deliver lectures each class period failures because they are trying their best to share information that they feel is valuable. I only wish young teachers could see the value in letting go of their need to *dominate* the classroom so that they could foster responsibility on the part of their students.

My students take *pride* in conducting interviews and inviting guest presenters. I stand back, plan, organize, and create a positive environment. Everyone who presents receives applause. We not only applaud for stars like Ms. Muncy and Mr. Slone but for students in class who have never spoken in front of a class before who step forward to unfold a grandmother's hand-pieced and hand-tacked quilt and tell a family story associated it.

Doug Aulick, you were on the right track, but those parents who came to class in place of their children had too much to offer to sit quietly at their children's desks.

Chapter Twenty-Three

Teaching is an ongoing process of rediscovering one's humility. The pride that comes from hearing your name respectfully spoken with a "Mr." included soon fades into distant memory when you stumble. During thirty years of teaching I have had my share of falls. How about the time I locked myself in the faculty restroom located in a busy hallway near my principal's office? Yes, there I was banging on the door like a fool and yelling loud enough to be heard in the principal's office nearby. He was the one who came to let me out as he mumbled something about the recent construction going on in the high school building and the doors and locks that did not work properly. There is a picture hidden in a closet shoebox. My wife swears it is me who stands beside Doug Ball, my biology teacher friend and former colleague. We are dressed in drag and being escorted by Jenny Jones, a student of ours and my Smith Avenue neighbor. My wife reminds me that we were dressed as women because we were participating in a pep rally for the girls' basketball team. What wearing a dress, a ladies' hat and carrying a purse had to do with school spirit, I now have no idea, but I vaguely remember not the embarrassment at the time but the principal's secretary who commented that I had nice legs. That Gallatin County High pep rally was difficult to live down!

Before that cross-dressing episode I suppose my greatest

embarrassment and dose of humility came when one of my students discovered a copy of Eastern Kentucky University's *Progress*, the university's yearbook. The picture inside of me was taken during my senior year of 1975, and my bell-bottomed trousers might have not been visible, but my long, Beatles-inspired hairstyle was there in all its glory. Those were the days of hair stylists. They nearly bankrupted small town barbers in the seventies. The university's Powell Student Center even included a stylist's shop downstairs near the bowling lanes. We were *too good* for small-town barbershops, or so we thought. So there I was standing beside Jody Fox, a fellow English major and honor student, with my hair hiding any trace of ears. I recall an EKU geology lab instructor who once walked by to check on my work and lifted my hair to make certain I could hear his remarks. He was not sure I had ears beneath all that hair.

These and many more embarrassing incidents exist somewhere in the closet of teachers' memories to remind us all of our progress toward humility. A poem by Wendell Berry "Thirty More Years" expresses this idea perfectly. As the narrator grows older, he grows smaller. In youth he thought himself large and important. As he grows older, he finds that he is small, not insignificant, but one among billions of God's creations.

My own journey toward humility was aided by a teaching experience I had on Big Sandy Community and Technical College's Prestonsburg campus. The local public school system's gifted and talented program bussed sixth grade students to our campus where they could take mini courses in subjects that were not available in the regular curriculum. I was asked to teach Spanish for one hour a day twice a week to a class of sixth-grade gifted and talented students from across the county. I intended the class to be a fun introduction to the language. We listened to Spanish songs by contemporary

222

entertainers like Selena, Ricky Martin, and Gloria Estefan and translated some of the lyrics into English. I used a whiteboard to introduce the young students to a small Spanish vocabulary, and I helped them pronounce the new vowel sounds and other sounds of the Spanish alphabet. We watched cartoons in Spanish and listened to commercials from Spanish radio and TV, commercials which advertised familiar products in familiar ways. A McDonald's commercial sounds the same in both languages, and the words are easily recalled as they are transposed from the target language. We did all the fun activities I could think of that had worked as Friday activities when I taught Spanish to high school students. I encouraged students to bring a pocket Spanish dictionary or a hand-held translator. I looked forward to the class, but keeping the attention of eleven-year-olds for sixty minutes at a time was not an easy task.

The last time I had taught eleven-year-olds Spanish was in a regular college classroom. As an experiment, our college invited gifted students to college to sit beside regular college students in my Spanish classes. In this teaching situation I had a great deal of help because the older college students, many of whom planned on becoming teachers themselves some day, took the children under their wings and helped with the instruction. The children helped the older students as well to lose their fear of speaking up and sounding stupid. Eleven-year-olds do not know the meaning of the word "fear."

I don't know how I found the time to be distracted from the task at hand—being alone with a group of thirty high-energy pre-adolescents, but I did. I had chosen to meet the class in the art gallery, located downstairs in the Magoffin Learning Resources Center because it was near the front entrance, close to restrooms, and the students would not disturb any classes on their way to and from the class. Most importantly, the art gallery was carpeted so that my students could sit comfortably crossed-legged on the floor. That seating arrangement made the class feel more informal. An added advantage was that students could view exhibits that would change from time to time.

When I teach, I am conscious of making the students feel as comfortable as possible. I suppose this goes back to some of my own uncomfortable experiences in junior high at Flat Gap School, sitting in classrooms that were heated only with coal stoves. I also make *myself* comfortable. Teachers teach better when they *feel* better. Some of my worst teachers were unhappy in another part of their lives or simply could not make themselves comfortable in front of a classroom. I never sit behind a teacher's desk, for example. I sit on top of it or on top of another flat surface in the room, and I don't stay there or any other place long. Instead, I walk around getting the attention of those who choose to sit far away from front and center. If I sit behind a desk at all, I sit in a student desk. I do this at times when I want students to discuss along with others and me and when I do not want to dominate that discussion with my own beliefs. When I test, I always move to the back of the classroom and sit in a student desk. I usually announce that my reason for doing so is simply to be more comfortable while not wasting time. I can get some grading or reading done. Some probably still feel that I am there to check for cheating, but I honestly rarely do so. I simply need to be comfortable while I do my work. When I confer with a student about a paper, I never face the student. I sit on the student's left side (I am right-handed) and read over the student's work first for content and then to help with writing mechanics. In the art gallery I put myself at ease by standing facing the piece of art or the photo that most captured my attention. This may sound distracting, but it was not.

One such painting that I was attracted to was a Tom Whitaker painting with the title *Humbleness*. I'll admit that I *did* become distracted from teaching, when I looked into the eyes of the man in this portrait. I was accustomed to landscapes and buildings and animals as subjects for Tom's art. I knew that Tom's fellow artist, Russell May, had seldom drawn people at all and that he was never happy with those people he had inserted into his settings. I had seen people in Tom's paintings before, but they had nearly always been part of a group, or from time to time, the person was Tom himself.

What made *Humbleness* unique then was that its subject was one man standing on his front porch. The screen door of his home framed him. He wore plastic-framed late-sixties-styled eyeglasses, and on his head was what I have always called an "old man's hat," a narrow brimmed hat—well worn and sweat stained. I felt drawn to the expression in the old man's eyes.

I believe the artist summed it up best by telling me of the subject, Mr. Prater, " He was known in his community as one who would give you the shirt off his back. He didn't have much, but he would offer you anything he had. He was always thinking of the well being of others, and although he was a storyteller, he was a different sort, for in his stories, *he* was never the central character. His world revolved around others whose ideas he respected and whose friendships he valued." Mr. Prater's humility shone in his eyes.

Tom Whitaker captured in those eyes a mountain trait that often goes misunderstood. Teaching the value of local culture involves first a discovery of what makes that culture unique. Humbleness is a respected quality in the mountain culture, one that mountain natives recognize at once. Tom illustrated humbleness through Mr. Prater's eyes. I did not know the man as Tom did, but I felt I knew him from the expression in those eyes.

Art and literature carry culture. They create, on the part of the observer or reader, an awareness of what makes individual cultures unique. Before I saw Tom's portrait of Mr. Prater, I had written my own version of the artist's message in a poem that I had also titled "Humbleness."

Two deaths were recently recorded in juxtaposition
In the national media.
After all, they occurred within days of each other
Worlds away.

Mother Teresa was buried in
Homespun muslin,
The simple white cloth she always wore.
All her life she strove to be poor.

The national media
Felt obligation to broadcast Mother's funeral,
Shamed to do so
By the days spent in tribute to a princess.

A world away from both lives
Mountain children are reminded
That greatest nobility through mountain generations
Has always been found in those who search for Christlike humbleness.

The poem includes a comparison of the media's treatment of two deaths and subsequent funerals: that of Princess Diana and of Mother Teresa. I mention the homespun muslin Mother Teresa always wore and write "All of her life she strove to be poor." My point, though, is to illustrate the difference in attention paid to the two deaths. The media was *shamed* into devoting coverage to Mother Teresa's passing because of the inordinate amount of attention they had devoted to writing and broadcasting every detail that could be discovered about the death of Princess Diana. I close the poem with a reference to my own culture and a tribute to Mother Teresa who visited east Kentucky and started an order in Letcher County that survives today to help the poor. Mountain children are taught the importance of the "Christlike humbleness" that Mother Teresa modeled throughout her life. In my poem I was illustrating, just as Tom did through his art, a quality of mountain people that often goes misunderstood.

Outsiders who come to live in the mountains remark that our people are too submissive and should speak with a louder voice about their problems and their achievements. Mountain children are taught that once they *announce* their achievements to the world, their achievements are diminished. A truly successful person does not display her or his success through clothing or cars or other possessions and certainly does not brag to the world by loudly announcing an achievement. To do so is to bring shame to the family who will quietly take pride in individual achievements but never broadcast accomplishments to the community. In a modern world where egos dominate, this cultural code may not seem progressive, but mountain people are slow to change, especially when a quality such as humility has been successfully passed through many generations.

I explained to Tom why I was drawn to his painting and bought the original before he had time to make numbered prints of the work. He sells originals, not because he has to, but because he has been provided sufficient reason to give up the piece. I take the painting to my classes each year as I read to my students my poem with the same title. Most nod and smile in recognition of a part of their culture they had taken for granted, a quality that makes them *different from* but not *better* than another from a different culture.

Mr. Prater has long ago passed away, but I see his son often. He walks, as do I, on the Kiwanis Trail at Paintsville Lake State Park. He knows how I feel about the portrait of his father because I have told him, but he carries with him always something more beautiful than even Tom's art—memories of his father's acts of kindness.

CHAPTER TWENTY-FOUR

Word of local writers has a way of making its way into the classroom once the teacher makes it known that those who write about local culture are valued models. That's how I met Sister Imogene Harless. Her teaching career took her from her West Virginia home across the river into Lawrence County and Martin County, Kentucky. She opened her two books of poetry for my classes and read with pride what she had been *given*.

Ms. Harless recalled for my students the day she began to take her writing seriously. She said the Lord asked her that day to look at her hands. "What do you have in your hands?" was the question she heard Him ask. "Why, Lord, I have nothing in my hands."
The Lord told her that something *should* be there. He went on to tell her to go gather up all the poems that she had scribbled on scraps of paper and left in piles around her home. She was to collect these poems and find a way to share them with others. From that day forward Ms. Harless began collecting poems for her first book and began looking for inspiration to write more. Her advice for my students was "Don't be lazy with your gift."

Before hearing the Lord speak to her about her writing, Ms. Harless would get an idea for a poem while lying in bed, but she was too lazy to get up, get a pen and a piece of paper and record her inspiration. She believed many were given the gift of creativity, but few did anything with the gift.

Ms. Harless had *loved* teaching. Her students became family to her. She loved to fish and remembered that young boys would often stop beside the road to lift rocks to find crawdads or dig fishing worms to bring to her to use as bait. She said she valued the quiet time alone she spent sitting on the bank of the creek waiting for the fish to bite. She would use this time to collect her thoughts about her day and plan for the next day of teaching.

Her other hobby was painting. She bashfully showed us some of her work. Her art was inspired by nature and captured the beauty of a foggy mountain morning or a red sunset, forecasting a morning shower. Her love for water permeated her art as well. One painting, though, she showed us with some shame. She had started it when she was hospitalized for "a little trouble I was having at the time." One nurse who hated her job had been mean to Ms. Harless, who admitted the tiniest of mean steaks as she showed us the little horned devil that she had inserted in her landscape drawing. She said she should have taken the devil, which represented the hateful nurse, out of the painting, but she had left it in for personal revenge.

Sister Harless last told us of the first story she remembered writing. During the forties, she attended a one-room school in her home county of Wayne in West Virginia. She had been in some kind of trouble at home with her parents and so wanted to do what all children at one time or another attempt to do—run away from home. Only she decided to make her escape through her imagination. In her story she built a giant slingshot and propelled herself all the way to the surface of the moon. Once there, she discovered that the moon was not so special a place as she had thought—no cheese or moon men—and besides, she missed her family, so she decided to return home. Oh, the view was nice. She could see all the way to the locks of the Big Sandy near Louisa, Kentucky. But the view was not worth the pain of homesickness she was feeling, so she sat on a cake of her mother's lye soap and rode back to Earth on a rainbow. On the way down, the soap shrunk causing her to "burn her britches." Otherwise she made it home safe and sound.

Ms. Harless' teacher read her story, but instead of encouraging her creativity, scolded her and explained that her story was impossible. She gave her a B, not the A Ms. Harless usually received. Imagine how vindicated Sister Harless felt when Neil Armstrong walked on the moon in 1969! She said she wished at that time that her teacher had still been living because she could have called to say, "I told you so."

I once heard James Still's reply when he was asked to define creativity. His words were, "I can't explain it. Nobody can. I just write what is in my head."

Silas House, a contemporary novelist from Lilly, Kentucky, in Laurel County, once attempted to define creativity by explaining that he writes at night in front of an open window while he listens to the night sounds. The "gift" *come*s to him. He cannot use his own handwriting to write what he has been given, for his words come to him so fast that through handwriting, he cannot get them down quickly enough. He uses the computer, typing hurriedly in order to allow the inspiration to flow from him onto the page. It is as if he is listening to a voice from inside his head. He feels as if a ghost is speaking to him. Silas House spoke to my students in March 2005, telling them this was especially true when he wrote *A Parchment of Leaves*. He listened to the voice and transposed. When he rereads some passages, he does not remember writing them. Sister Imogene Harless would understand.

When I decided to *not* "be lazy with my gift," I first needed to discover whether my writing might appeal to a wider audience than my children and my wife, I did so in a quiet, secretive way. Our college's president, Dr. Henry A. Campbell, Jr., encouraged faculty to help in any way we could when Elderhostel groups would visit Floyd County's Jenny Wiley State Park. I taught Spanish and writing in those days, and he would suggest that I teach a conversational Spanish class. I decided instead that I would make copies of some of my poems and take them to read to this audience made up of many retired teachers and college professors. I had no confidence that anyone would like my writing other than family, but I realized that these were strangers whom I would likely never see again. Just in case they did not enjoy my poems, I took along my guitar. I sing and play Bluegrass a little. Also I took along a video about east Kentucky from the TBS "Portrait of America" documentary hosted by Hal Holbrook which begins with a quote from former Kentucky governor, A. B. "Happy" Chandler: "I never met a Kentuckian who wasn't going home." Jean Ritchie, the internationally famous folksinger from Perry County closes the piece with "You can go home again, and I've done it. I have traveled all over the world, and I love it here." The narrator refers to coal miners as "people who can afford the luxury of remaining in east Kentucky." This was the first time I had ever seen anything nationally telecast that positively reflected our culture.

My students can relate to the rest of my story. I knew whether my singing had touched my audience because as I sang, I made eye contact and sometimes saw tears or smiles. While I was reading my poems to the Elderhostel participants, I was looking down and so was not able to read their reactions. When I finished reading, I would pretend to take a long while to pack up my materials while declining the offers of staff at the state park to help me get my belongings to my truck. I would leave the conference room but pretend to have forgotten something so that I could return. Once I was alone, I would check the garbage cans to see if my poems had been thrown away or kept. I knew if my audience members *kept* the poems, they must have liked them at least a little. Later on as my confidence rose, I would actually listen to those who stayed behind to tell me how much they had enjoyed a particular poem or to ask me if they could purchase a book of my poems. We all tend to dismiss compliments and remember criticisms, and so did I at first. I had chosen my audience of strangers deliberately. If they did not like my writing, I had little to lose. The fact that they did not know me made their compliments easier to accept as well. I had successfully read to a mature, educated audience, and many had enjoyed hearing and reading my poems. I'm sure my writing improved along with my confidence. Hearing my "garbage can" story illustrates the importance of considering the audience and gives my students hope that they too might gain confidence in their own writing abilities by reading before an audience.

CHAPTER TWENTY-FIVE

Since 1980 when I used my first Apple II computer in the classroom, I have been an advocate for the use of technology in the classroom. In those days computers were little more than game gadgets, but the folks at Apple soon realized that if they could provide learning software, teachers would become customers. Also through exposure to computers at school, students would go home and ask Mom and Dad to buy one. This early selling strategy accounts for Apple's role in the initial boom in the personal computer industry. These first computers we used at Gallatin County High did not even have word processing capability. Due to Apple's education-sales strategy, software was available from the beginning though. Such software could help students build a better foreign language vocabulary or improve grammar and punctuation skills.

The custodian at our school, Mr. Lykins, a native of Magoffin County, liked me because I was from the mountains, so he built for me two cabinets to hold the Apple computers that I purchased for my classroom. These cabinets were functional—complete with hinged plywood doors that could swing shut and lock when I was not in the room. I remember that as many as five or six students could stand behind the open cabinet doors, view the screen and enjoy completing games and exercises together. Part of the excitement could be attributed to newness of the technology, but part also resulted from students' discovery of a new way to use a keyboard and screen.

With age comes speculation, and several years later when the Internet came along, I was skeptical as to whether it could benefit my students. I am ashamed to admit it now, but I did not allow my students to use the Internet for completing research in those early days. I insisted that they use books as sources as I had when I was in school and viewed the Internet as a source of generally bad information and advertising.

Of course, I have since discovered that I was both correct and incorrect. The Internet *can be* a source of misinformation, pop-up advertising, and Spam e-mail, but it is also a resource tool for education and information retrieval. Students and teachers simply must learn where to look. Search engines such as GOOGLE, edu sites, org sites, NPR archives, on-line library collections, as well as journalistic sites such as USA.Today.com make the Internet indispensable to educators and students alike.

Soon after my *conversion* to the Internet, Debbie Daniels, technology coordinator and supervisor of instruction for the Floyd County Board of Education, asked me whether I would consider teaching Spanish again to high school students. I would be hired to teach an on-line course. I could work primarily on evenings and weekends. I had missed teaching Spanish, so though skeptical that Spanish could be taught as an Internet course, I said yes. I then was scheduled to attend an on-line workshop in Frankfort at the state department of education.

During the workshop, I remained skeptical throughout the presentation of the software and course content until we were shown the program Pure Voice—a sort of Real Player intended for use in foreign language instruction. The idea was that I could hear my students' voices on recordings they uploaded to me via the Internet. I could, in turn, respond with my own written comments or my own Pure Voice recording, demonstrating the correct pronunciation. "This can be the missing link in communication that I have been concerned would be lacking in the course," I thought.

My first group of students was located at South Floyd High. They were to meet for fifty minutes each day, work on course assignments that they would send to me via e-mail, and study the accompanying textbooks on their own in order to be able to do on-line activities which would be graded week-by-week by me.

At first my students demonstrated the same enthusiasm that I had seen years before when students were first introduced to the old Apple computers. As the class progressed though, I began to receive more and more panicked comments from the facilitator who sat in with the students. She was an aide who knew no Spanish but had been assigned to monitor students and make sure they did their work. She felt helpless and alone without the training she needed. I felt helpless as well because I could not step in to help students who became lost. Several students did well, at least in the beginning, and the class was set up to encourage bright students to discover Spanish basics and even move on to investigate websites filled with Spanish vocabulary. All the technology in the world will help students only if they are *motivated* to learn. Few students can self-motivate. Even the best and brightest need inspiration and encouragement from time to time.

Near the end of the first semester, the "glow" of technology began to fade. I was reduced to patting the few successful students on the back while rewarding them with As and scolding students who made half-hearted efforts or who did not bother to complete their assignments. Even students who were able to motivate themselves without a teacher present could have learned so much more with a teacher in the classroom.

Ironically, I think of the one-room-school classroom as I consider on-line teaching. In one-room schools there was a community of learners who supported each other in the learning process. Students who needed extra help learned from overhearing lessons taught to others, and students could also help one another one-on-one. Building such a close community of on-line learners is a difficult challenge.

All Kentucky Virtual High School classes are monitored at the State Department of Education offices in Frankfort. Although I was beginning to have my doubts about on-line teaching, the consultants at the KVHS saw the work I was putting into individual lessons for the students at South Floyd High and asked me to take on another class. These students were enrolled at a Catholic high school in Maysville, Kentucky. Their on-line teacher had resigned. I was assured that the principal and the parents wholeheartedly supported the class and that the private school had employed a Spanish-speaking native to come in three days a week to help students with their pronunciation. As I said, I was becoming more and more skeptical but had not yet given up on the prospect of reaching students over the Internet, so I said yes.

As the spring semester progressed, I discovered that what the principal, the parents and the facilitator wanted from me was enough busy work to keep these energetic high school freshmen on task for five hours each week. I also soon discovered that these students and their parents would not be happy unless the students received the As they had become accustomed to whether or not their work was deserving of the grade. Students would hurry through their assignments, often using translators, anything to finish the work.

237

They did not care whether they learned anything or not.

As I have discussed my on-line teaching experience with colleagues, I find that they have discovered that only the best and brightest mature college students excel in on-line classes. The self-motivation required to do well and learn in these classes is simply not present in high school students and is sometimes not present in traditional college students.

A state government program once created never dies, so I assume that the Kentucky Virtual High School state department of education employees will go on delivering busy work to students in exchange for the praise that too often comes from making use of whatever is *new* technology-wise.

I believe in the "coincidences" or *signs* that James Still's daughter talked about believing in. In Frankfort on the morning of my first meeting concerning teaching Internet classes, I ran into one of my old teachers from Flat Gap. He was catching an elevator in the Kentucky State Office Tower. When he learned of my reason for being there, he expressed reservations about offering on-line classes to high school students. I should have listened. I missed my *sign*. It could not have been more clearly delivered to me, but I missed it. I should have gone home. Instead, I spent a year learning what Mr. Burchett already knew from a long career in education and what Jesse Stuart and Cratis Williams knew from their experience teaching in one-room schools: The best learning occurs from the interaction of a teacher and students *inside* the classroom.

CHAPTER TWENTY-SIX

While I was away from the mountains earning a graduate degree and teaching English and Spanish to northern Kentucky students, the US Army Corps of Engineers was busy building a dam for a flood control project four miles west of my hometown. Paint Creek flooding came as regularly as springtime in Johnson County. Paintsville Lake began impounding water from Little Paint Creek on September 19, 1981. By 1984, when I came home to teach in the mountains, the lake was doing its job of preventing flooding, making way for residential and commercial development on land that had been in the flood plain as I grew up, as well as providing a 1,140 acre recreational waterway.

Since 1977, in the spring of my second year of teaching, I have chosen to live near water. In Warsaw, on the Ohio River, I would push my son's stroller along the street adjacent to the river so that we could see sunset's colors on the current rippled surface. I soon discovered Harlan Hubbard's work *Shantyboat* and dreamed of Johnboats and shantyboats and drifting to the confluence of the Ohio and Mississippi Rivers. I fished for catfish from a canoe in the Ohio's backwater. Our favorite restaurant, the Key West Shrimp House, was located in Madison, Indiana, just across the bridge from Trimble County, Kentucky, the location of Harlan and Anna Hubbard's river-overlook home. As I crossed the bridge from Milton to Madison, my thoughts would turn to the famous northern Kentucky writer and artist whose home was around the river's bend.

I proposed to my wife while seated in a glassed-in front- room table at the Key West Shrimp House overlooking the Ohio River. When her time came to deliver our first child, I drove Debbie to Saint Elizabeth's Hospital in Covington, Kentucky alongside the part of the Ohio that US Route 42 borders in Gallatin County. Somehow I was relaxed long enough to see the reflection of a full moon on the quiet river's surface as I drove northeast. The hospital itself was set high on a hill so that I could see through the atrium glass the river winding below, dividing the city of Cincinnati from Covington and Newport, Kentucky.

On Saturday mornings, we would drive across Markland Dam to the small river town of Vevay, Indiana, and the closest grocery store. We would often take the time to stop and climb the steps to the Ohio River overlook. Sometimes riverboats like the *Delta Queen* were locking through. We loved to listen to its signature calliope. If a riverboat were not present, there would almost always be a loaded river barge hauling fuel or coal downstream toward Louisville and points beyond. In the winter of 1977, the river froze completely over in some places, preventing barge traffic and creating a surreal scene not duplicated in the almost thirty years since that record winter.

The timing of the impoundment of Paintsville Lake coincided perfectly with my returning to teach at Prestonsburg Community College, but upon my return, the first body of water I rediscovered with my family was Dewey Lake in Floyd County's Jenny Wiley State Park. My great aunt Adda, my grandfather Slone's sister, was caretaker of Sandy Valley Girl Scout Camp. From her cabin home I saw newly impounded Dewey Lake for the first time when I was four. As a boy my father would drive us to Dewey Lake on Sunday afternoons. A road ran parallel to one side of the lake all the way from the dam to May Lodge. Gravel pull-offs on the lake side of the road allowed drivers to stop for views of the water or for picnics.

Near the water I always felt at home. Summers on my grandparents' farm I would fish and swim in the creek, or when the summer rains did not sufficiently fill the creek for swimming, I would go wading. Those times when my grandmother and mother would kick off their shoes and go wading with me are special memories.

The memory of sitting in my father's car beside Dewey Lake is not a special one. In my mind I associate it with pain and with feeling poor. One Sunday afternoon Dad had opened his car door as the family sat parked, looking out at the boaters and water skiers. As usual I was seated directly behind him in the back seat where I recall I would often stare into his eyes through the rear-view mirror. If they showed happiness, we would be in store for a pleasant ride. I must have been daydreaming or looking at the sparkling stars of reflected sunlight that appear on the water's surface as the sun lowers in the sky, for I did not notice my father slamming his door shut in time to get my hand out of the way. My thumb still bears the scar.

When I was old enough to drive, I could never enjoy, as did my friends, parking alongside the lake to steal a kiss from my girlfriend on the way to the Sky View Drive-In Movie Theatre because I associated those gravel overlooks with pain. Those late Sunday afternoons are also memories of what it felt like to be poor. Boats with skiers crowded and churned the lake's surface with their wakes. I dreamed of what it would be like to be *on* the lake and not *beside* it. I realized that this dream was somehow tied to education and that with a college degree I might some day have enough extra money to afford a boat.

Soon after moving home to the mountains, my family and I

discovered a walking trail whose entrance was near Dewey Dam. The trail/road bed provided several wonderful views of the lake and came with no old memories attached because I never knew about the trail when I was growing up nearby. I pushed my son in a stroller as we enjoyed walking the old access road to old natural gas wells, which led past old Native American burial grounds. The trail was not a looping one, so when we became tired, we would turn to retrace our steps back to the dam. We would pack sandwiches, water, and chocolate chip cookies to enjoy on our way back.

My wife and I were both teaching. We eventually sold our old home in Warsaw and had a little extra money, so I decided the time was right to enjoy both Dewey and Paintsville Lakes with the purchase of my first boat. I needed help. Other than a canoe I had never been in a boat. I had no idea how to operate one or how to even get it into the water for that matter. I chose a small fifteen-feet long bass boat with a Johnson forty-eight horsepower outboard motor and an electric trolling motor mounted in the front beside a bow-mounted fishing seat. Luckily the salesman at Collie's Marine in Pikeville where I purchased the boat delivered it to Paintsville Lake and offered to give me my first lesson in launching and operating it. He even gave me fishing tips as he pointed out his favorite places to fish, old roadbeds that had been submerged when the lake filled with water.

I was too scared to listen closely to the salesman's fish tales. I remember holding tightly to the side of the little boat as we likely reached a speed of no more than thirty miles an hour. It felt like *flying* to me.

After a week of admiring the boat in my driveway, I decided I had enough nerve to take my family on their first adventure on Paintsville Lake. The small Johnson outboard did not have power tilt and trim, so after putting the boat into the water and making sure that everyone was seated safely with their life jackets on, I had to remember to walk to the stern to tilt the motor down deeper into the water. My wife sat in the passenger's seat clutching our baby daughter who wore her own tiny life jacket complete with a handle for pulling her out of the water in case she fell in. As we picked up speed, the bow of the boat never lowered. The boat could not level or "plane" off because the motor's lower unit was at the wrong angle. I had forgotten to lower the motor. As the bow lifted higher and higher out of the water, my wife's screams grew louder. I finally realized what I had forgotten, but Debbie and my son and daughter never relaxed on that boat after that. I knew that I had not chosen a family boat and that if we were going to ever enjoy our time on the water, we would need a different boat.

At Dave's Marine Sales in Kenova, West Virginia, we found a larger boat that we could afford. It was a Bayliner deep vee bow-rider styled boat complete with forward and rear facing seats for four. Most importantly it was large enough so that Debbie could not touch water, so she could feel safe inside. This boat came with no deliveryman or first lesson, but I was able to manage with the benefit of the experience I had gained from handling the little fishing boat. Most important of all, the motor came with power tilt and trim—no more walking to the back of the boat to lower the motor into the water by hand.

We soon decided to leave the boat in the water in a rented Marina slip. The convenience of being able to just step on board the boat and within ten minutes being out on the lake has made all the difference. Our time on the water has made us closer as a family. When I take the boat out alone and return to the marina, I find myself giving excuses to other boaters who ask, "How many did you catch?"

because I usually do not fish. I find waterfalls in laurel coves and take in the smells, sights, and sounds of nature, or I read or listen to distant radio stations and to National Public Radio.

My own best teachers have taught me with words or through their own examples that good teachers find a way to be happy outside the classroom. Not only do they enjoy teaching, but they also enjoy faith, family, and life away from teaching. Dr. Cratis Williams, who began his teaching in a Lawrence County one-room school and went on to become a professor and administrator at Appalachian State University, once said that when he had a bad day teaching, it was *his* fault for staying up too late or out too late the night before. He realized the energy level required to teach and the need to rest and prepare oneself for the day ahead. For me that preparation is best done on water. In the evenings now I take out on the lake the pontoon boat we keep at the marina and go searching for deer, wild turkeys, otters, or great blue herons. I motor slowly into a different sunset each evening. I find that when I am rested and relaxed, I can more easily create a relaxed atmosphere in my classroom. Once I overheard a student describing my literature class to another. She said, "Taking his class is like taking time out in the afternoon for a cup of tea." A teacher who has taken time to be rested and happy outside the classroom first can then create a classroom atmosphere that facilitates learning.

From Hood's Creek wading and diving into swimming holes, to Big Sandy River bank fishing for catfish, to dreaming from the back seat of my father's lakeside parked car, to watching Ohio River boats and barges, and finally to boating on my mountain lake, I have always loved being near water. I am a better teacher because I realize enjoying what I love outside the classroom is an important part of my preparation for teaching.

CHAPTER TWENTY-SEVEN

Lately I have been discovering the connectivity of all that has occurred and is occurring in my life. Think about it. Events that happened years ago now seem to have been written for each of us, not as haphazard episodes but as important parts of a larger story. When I was younger, I thought of life (as I'm sure my twenty-three year-old son does) as a series of unconnected experiences that happened by chance. At age twenty-three I would never have believed someone who told me that my life story had an outline and that its organization would be clear to me some day.

When I was a little boy, I would be asked to sit at the hospital bedside of my grandmother Slone to keep her company and to fetch the nurse or to bring her things she needed. I would take along a model car kit to help time pass more quickly. Once in a while the kit would come boxed without printed instructions. Only when I managed to nearly finish putting the pieces together, would I begin to see how each piece played its role in the finished product. I could then understand the reason I had needed to do things in the correct order. For example, I learned from experience to put the engine together first. There would usually be five parts. The oil pan was glued on first. Then the two valve covers—chrome plated if you were lucky—were glued onto the top of each set of cylinder heads. The assembly required care because each valve cover had its set of pins on the bottom for guiding the parts into place. It was important not to break any of these pins by rushing the job or forcing the parts together. Next came the carburetor—almost never chrome—and on top of it the round air cleaner was glued. I could put the engine together from memory. I had learned the importance of putting together the engine and setting it aside to dry for later attachment to the car's frame. It had to fit correctly, or the body would not fit snugly on the frame. I recall several cars that when completed would have hoods forever raised one quarter of an inch because I had not assembled the engine or attached it to the frame correctly.

Why, as a young man, I could not see my own life as a model car kit without instructions is a mystery to me today. Every piece of my life and my teaching career has had its unique purpose. I just couldn't see how the pieces fit together when I was young. I guess we all do pretty well considering we don't have access to the plans/instructions God intentionally leaves out of our "boxes."

The year was 1970. Mr. Brewer announced that our high school band would be performing at a groundbreaking ceremony for a rehabilitation center to be built at Thelma, Kentucky, in my home county. I had no way of knowing that this center would some day play such an important role in the lives of my students.

The Carl D. Perkins Comprehensive Rehabilitation Center in Johnson County has the mission of providing services to individuals with disabilities so they may achieve suitable employment and independence. The center accepts students aged sixteen or older who have survived injuries that have added challenges to their lives. In addition to offering physical, occupational, speech, and language rehabilitation therapy, the center's therapists and teachers help students learn vocational skills in order to be able to return to jobs they left behind or to learn skills required for new career opportunities. Some students have the strong desire to achieve their college degrees, so the center provides transportation so that they can attend Big Sandy Community and Technical College.

Seeing a quadriplegic wheel in to a college classroom must have caused me considerable panic early in my college teaching career. Now upon seeing the chair, I smile, knowing that this class will have the influence of still another inspirational student and story.

When handicapped students are non-traditional in terms of age as well, my smile widens, for I have learned to value older students' participation in my classes. This must have come early on in the "putting together" of my teaching experience when Jan Cook and Barbara Chandler walked into my first class in Prestonsburg.

Soon non-traditional students with disabilities from all over Kentucky began arriving in my classes. Ginger Burns from Carroll County in northern Kentucky would wheel her chair into room 114 and confidently read papers reflecting her determination to succeed at anything she attempted. An auto accident caused by a deer running out in front of her had resulted in her injuries. She asked for help only rarely and attended because she wanted to learn, not because attendance was required. I had lived in the county adjacent to hers, and before and after class we would talk about old friends and about changes occurring with the coming of a NASCAR racetrack nearby and the construction of gambling casinos on the Indiana side of the Ohio River. Some days Ginger had a difficult time supporting her own head, but her spirit was like the river near where she was born. The strength of its current never wavered.

Tom Prewitt came to my class in the fall of 2003. I remember he asked me to announce to the other students that the college would pay for someone to help him get his things unpacked and packed and take notes for him. Almost immediately a student named Sheila

Prater set about doing what was required with very little instruction. Her sister had been a certified nurses' assistant, and Sheila was attending Big Sandy Community and Technical College in order to become a registered nurse. Sheila took no money from the college to help Tom. She helped him because she *wanted to*—the same reason she is going to be a fine nurse some day very soon. I joked with Tom about paying her just before the Christmas break, and I do think I shamed him into giving her a Christmas present. He and I took Sheila for granted. She helped me as much as she did Tom. A challenge of mine is getting students to volunteer to read their papers aloud. Sheila was always first to volunteer to read her papers with pride and poise, showing younger students just how it should be done.

It's sometimes not apparent to my handicapped students that they have a twofold purpose for being at my college. They are not only returning to college to complete their studies and receive their degrees, but also to *give* of themselves to others. Peers who have been selfish all their lives and who believe that life owes *them* everything, do a great deal of growing up while listening to students like Ginger Burns and Tom Prewitt.

I encouraged Tom to write about the story of his accident. I know writing can be therapy. In this case I knew that the therapy, although unnecessary for Tom himself, might help others—a lesson in determination and faith that might inspire them to change something about their own lives. He called the paper "The Day That Changed My Life Forever."

One "pristine" Saturday morning, Tom was staying at his aunt and uncle's cabin in Laurel County not far from the Cumberland River. The cabin was located inside the Daniel Boone National Forest about midway between Lake Cumberland and Laurel Lake near the "town" of Bald Rock where there was only one country store,

Morgan's Grocery. Tom and his brother enjoyed four-wheeling on some nearby trails. On one such trail they drove for about a half mile and discovered that it "snaked" down to the Cumberland River. The water level was down so they could ride along the banks and play in the mud a little. Tom was in the lead as they started back up into the woods in search of another trail when suddenly a little low bank appeared in front of him. He remembered seeing his brother drive right on through the area, but Tom's first attempt failed, resulting in loss of traction and spinning tires. When he tried the second time, he was aware of the tires starting to spin again, and the next thing he knew he heard a crunch and felt his body go numb. He knew instantly that his neck was broken. His brother began to panic, but Tom calmly told him that the damage was already done: "Why I think I was so calm was because God was there with me helping me get through."

Since Tom couldn't feel anything, he couldn't feel the weight of the eight-hundred-fifty-pound four-wheeler on top of him. Adrenaline flowing, his little brother and two riverbank fishermen lifted the four-wheeler off of him. Then one of them left to go to the boat dock to call for help. Tom is not sure how long he lay there, but he does remember smoking at least three or four cigarettes before the fisherman and the paramedics arrived back at the scene of the accident. He was put on a pontoon to be taken down river to the marina. Then he was taken by ambulance to an open area where a medivac helicopter landed to fly him to the UK Medical Center, the nearest medical center with a trauma care unit. He recalled a dream he had while unconscious: "I dreamed that people like used car dealers were bidding for my soul and that I was in another world." When later told that he had gone "code blue," he knew the dream made sense.

Tom is now a rehabilitating quadriplegic trying to start over in a new life: "The man who was once a well-paid railroad engineer is now with you in this classroom trying to do whatever it takes to make a new life for myself and just maybe help someone not to take life for granted like I did. In lieu of all that I have done since my accident, I still have a long row to hoe ahead…. Be grateful for the little things because they can be gone just like that."

Tom's words inspired, but they pale in comparison to the inspiration his actions provided young students in his class. He attended in spite of the pain from the bedsores that periodically sent him into the hospital. If *he* could overcome the obstacles that life had delivered, then they could achieve their own dreams, and perhaps like Sheila they too could offer a helping hand to someone else along the way.

As I stood in an open field playing the tuba at the groundbreaking ceremony for the Carl D. Perkins Comprehensive Rehabilitation Center, I had no idea the center would help thousands of students transition into different lives. By sending students to my college classroom, the center has offered lessons to thousands more who have had the good fortune to be blessed with classmates like Ginger and Tom.

CONCLUSION

The Big Sandy Valley in the mountains of east Kentucky has been the birthplace of many talented teachers and writers— models for those who will follow in their footsteps. James Still died on Saturday, April 28, 2001, sixty-nine days short of his 95th birthday. In his hospital bed during the days prior to his death, he was working on a manuscript about his boyhood. During his illness the number of books he read each week *increased*. In the interview conducted months before he died, Mr. Still expressed his concern that teachers might lose their love for reading. It was his hope that teachers never stop reading and that they continue to instill in their students the love of books. Contemporary writer Silas House's seventh grade teacher Sandra Stidham gave him a copy of Harper Lee's novel *To Kill a Mockingbird*. Reading this novel changed his life forever.

A college degree marks the *beginning* of a lifetime of learning. By encouraging students' love for reading, introducing them to model writers, and helping them form their own writing community, teachers can help students develop reading habits that, like Mr. Still's, may last a lifetime. They may even inspire a future writer just as Silas House's teacher did.

Mr. Still was determined to get books into the hands of children. He would often recount the story of how books had changed his own life. His goal was to inspire young people to love reading.

Today's teachers have the opportunity to introduce their students to the tremendous wealth of writers, like Mr. Still, who are connected to their place as he was and who, through their writing, are affirming the importance of family, community, and cultural heritage.

Not long ago, at Porter Elementary School where my wife Debbie teaches, the Lexington Children's Theatre performed an adaptation of James Still's classic children's book, *Jack and the Wonder Beans*. Several teachers borrowed our copy of the book in order to read it to their students before the play was to be presented. They enjoyed introducing their young students to an author who loved writing for children as much as for adults—one who wrote books filled with the language, rhythm, and culture of the mountains.

My students today do not understand the reason, but in most every college writing or literature class I teach, I take a book along just as I'm sure Mr. Still would have done. As I tell them about the writer, I let my students pass the book around the classroom. I smile when I see a student write the name of the book in his or her notebook or take the time to read the preface. Recently a student said he had read Billy C. Clark's *A Long Row to Hoe* after discovering the classic autobiography in my classroom. As he was telling me how much he enjoyed Mr. Clark's work, I was thinking about the fact that even though Brad has a job and children to support as he is attending my college, he is *determined* to obtain his degree. He intends to teach English some day. I know he will introduce his students to Billy Clark's autobiography because he has found his own *To Kill a Mockingbird*.

Mrs. Bernice Ferguson, my third grade teacher, introduced me to Dr. Arville Wheeler's *White Squaw*, the story of Jenny Wiley. She read the book aloud to her students. I listened with my eyes closed, my head down, and my imagination soaring. Mrs. Ferguson kindled a lifetime love of reading.

I recently had a conversation with Bill Duke, one of the first teachers who inspired me to pursue a teaching career, as he and I were walking on a trail near Paintsville Lake. Mr. Duke introduced me to the work of Jesse Stuart. He was my freshman English teacher at Flat Gap High School during the '67/'68 school year. Upon learning that I was writing a book about teaching, Mr. Duke was genuinely pleased. I thought at first he was happy for *me*—happy that I was near the completion of a three-year project. When I had time to further reflect, I understood the true reason Mr. Duke was pleased. I recalled what Jesse Stuart had to say about teaching: "Good teaching is forever, and the teacher is immortal." Mr. Duke was pleased to know that *his* teaching had lived on through one of his former students.

One of my current students, while doing a research paper for me, recently interviewed Anna Stepp, a former student of mine who is principal of Warfield Elementary School in Martin County. Anna sent me a note saying that she remembered my teaching and telling me how much she had enjoyed teaching young people herself.

Mr. Duke, Mrs. McKenzie, Mrs. Ross, Mrs. Ferguson, Miss Wallen, Mr. Lagos, Dr. Fontana, and all my former teachers who *loved* their profession are still living in my classroom today. They opened the door to my own lifetime of learning.

Mr. Duke, you will receive that copy of the book I promised you. Let it be your own personal note of thanks as well as a reminder that your teaching will always live on through your students.

ABOUT THE AUTHOR

Ken Slone's collection of poetry, *At Home in the Mountains,* was published in 2001 by the Jesse Stuart Foundation and is ready for its third printing. His new book, *Mountain Teacher,* is an autobiography featuring stories illustrating the importance of building a community in the classroom, true stories that span a thirty-year teaching career. After earning his graduate degree from Xavier University in Cincinnati, Ohio, he returned in 1984 to his home county of Johnson where he lives today with his wife Debbie and daughter and son, Beth and Stephen. Ken is professor of English at Big Sandy Community and Technical College where he received the Great Teacher Award in 1999 for teaching his students to take pride in their Appalachian heritage and to write from their hearts.

Martin Student Center Prestonsburg campus
Big Sandy Community and Technical College